Small Staff Association Fundamentals

Executive Editor
JIMELLE F. RUMBERG, CAE

ASAE & THE CENTER FOR ASSOCIATION LEADERSHIP

The authors have worked to ensure information in this book is accurate as of the time of publication and consistent with standards of good practice in the general management community. As research and practice advance, however, standards may change. For this reason, it is recommended that readers evaluate the applicability of any recommendation in light of particular situations and changing standards.

American Society of Association Executives
1575 I Street, NW
Washington, DC 20005-1103
Phone: (202) 626-2723; (888) 950-2723 outside the metropolitan Washington, DC area
Fax: (202) 408-9633
E-mail: books@asaenet.org
ASAE's core purpose is to advance the value of voluntary associations to society and to support the professionalism of the individuals who lead them.

Susan Robertson, Senior Vice President, Marketing and Communications
Keith Skillman, Vice President of Publications and Editorial Director
Baron Williams, Director of Book Publishing

Editor: Sandra R. Sabo, Mendota Heights, MN
Cover and interior design: Cimarron Design, www.cimarrondesign.com

This book is available at a special discount when ordered in bulk quantities. For information, contact the ASAE Member Service Center at (202) 371-0940.

A complete catalog of titles is available on the ASAE Web site at
www.asaenet.org/bookstore

Contents

Contributors

Trudy Aron, CAE
Executive Director, Kansas Chapter of the American Institute of
Architects, Topeka
Past Chairman, ASAE Small Staff Advisory Committee

Diana Ewert, CAE
Senior Manager of State Government Relations, Washington Office,
American Academy of Family Physicians, Leawood, Kansas
Member, ASAE Small Staff Advisory Committee

Tom Holt, CAE
Executive Director, Oregon State Pharmacy Association, Wilsonville

Robert E. McLean, CAE
President, REM Association Services, Arlington, Virginia
Member, ASAE Small Staff Advisory Committee

Sharon K. Mellor, CAE
Executive Director, American Academy of Periodontology, Chicago,
Illinois

Shirley L. Nimsky
Executive Director, International Society of Endovascular Specialists,
Phoenix, Arizona
2004–05 Chairman, ASAE Small Staff Advisory Committee

Jimelle F. Rumberg, CAE
Executive Director, West Virginia Psychological Association, Charleston
Member, ASAE Small Staff Advisory Committee

Dana Saal, CAE
Convention Coordinator, Illinois State Veterinary Medical Association, Springfield

Kim B. Stoneking, CAE
Executive Director, Indiana Association of Insurance and Financial Advisors, Indianapolis
2005–06 Chairman, ASAE Small Staff Advisory Committee

Peter S. Weber, CAE
Executive Director, Illinois State Veterinary Medical Association, Springfield
Member, ASAE Small Staff Advisory Committee

Introduction

By Jimelle F. Rumberg, CAE

Welcome to the world of being an association executive!

Business, trade, or professional management success does not automatically equate to achievement in the arena of association management. Success in for-profit business is measured by profits, while success in nonprofit associations relates to member benefits and perceived intangibles, such as belonging to a member-community or benevolence. And, for some members, belonging to your association is prestigious or necessary for a professional resume. As an association executive, you must multi-task administratively and cater to the differing needs of these various members to be successful.

It's key to quickly get up to speed and assimilate into your new association. In the beginning, it is perfectly acceptable—and expected—that you will lean on the board of directors. Talk with the executive committee or officers of the board, asking for their input and the institutional history, before developing your final decisions. These elected leaders will appreciate your asking for and valuing their opinions.

Because managing an association is a unique job, however, volunteers won't be able to supply all the information you need. That's where this book comes in. It's written primarily for newly hired chief executives of small nonprofit associations (although it will be a useful resource for staff members of all association sizes).

More specifically, this primer is focused on the needs of the new executive managing an organization with an annual budget of $100,000 of less—someone who has to do it all with a limited budget, with little or no staff, and with little or no association experience.

First Things First

As the new executive—especially if you have no staff—first insist upon having a financial audit performed. If you are working with the association's finances, also acquire bonding insurance. These steps will not only protect you and the association but also show your integrity as an executive.

If you are the executive of a 501(c)(6) state organization and intend to speak to or socialize with any legislators within your state in an official capacity, register as a lobbyist. A 501(c)(3) organization cannot lobby per se, so confirm your association's IRS designation and act accordingly. If you don't know whether your association is a 501(c)(3) or 501(c)(6), call the IRS and ask for a replacement letter of determination.

Place the letter in a special reference file, along with copies of previous IRS Form 990s (Return of Organization Exempt From Income Tax), if available. The IRS can also address other questions that may arise—for example, are you an employee or an independent contractor? (You'll find an online test and other resources at www.irs.gov.)

Also review the association's Articles of Incorporation. If you cannot locate these, contact the Secretary of State's office in your state or the one in which your association was incorporated when formed. This office—which may have a different name in your state—usually renews your business license as well. Place a copy of the Articles of Incorporation in the special reference file.

Above all, read your association's bylaws. In fact, make it a habit to read them before every board meeting so you aren't derailed or embarrassed by ignorance. It's your job to know what's in the association bylaws and to address questions regarding their contents.

The Realities

The first and foremost rule of association management is: "No one is more important to an association then its members." Your ability to get along with the internal and external community is paramount.

Not only the board but also rank-and-file members will closely scrutinize your organizational and administrative abilities, not to mention your integrity and devotion to the association's mission. They will mentally assess these items when it comes time to write the check for dues, assessments, or gifts. You, as the executive, become the "face" of the association both publicly and professionally. Your leadership should enhance and complement the association, not destroy it.

As the staff executive, you must be highly ethical and never manipulative. Respect your members and your staff, and help your volunteers and staff give their services to benefit the group. Always remember you cannot command—only suggest, propose, and listen. Your authority is not yours but the board's, and you serve at the board's will. In all situations, be diplomatic, gracious, empathetic, and reassuring. The members and staff will look to you for guidance. Never be hasty in judgment, always be generous, and practice the Golden Rule.

Here are some additional suggestions:

Read, read, read. This enables you to stay on top of your game as an association executive—especially if you read up on areas in which you fall short. For example, weaknesses in associations can almost always be traced to some inadequacy of their executives' leadership abilities, so don't hesitate to hit the books on this important topic.

Wear the best you can afford. Yes, the old saying is true: "Clothes make the person." You don't need a closet full of new clothes every season, but at the least purchase a new pair of shoes and one new jacket, tie, or blouse.

Since you *are* the association, you need to dress and act the part. Be aware that you are being visually assessed by everyone you meet—and that first impression is a lasting one. So polish your shoes routinely. Use a nice pen when attending meetings, and carry a presentable portfolio and daily planner. While leather is a classic choice for executive accessories, vinyl may be your only option; just make sure it's a nice quality vinyl portfolio, not a dog-eared cardboard clipboard.

Mind your manners. You can find many good business tips in etiquette books, such as those written by Letitia Baldridge, Amy Vanderbilt, or Emily Post. You'll get a refresher course, for example, on giving a toast, writing personal notes of bereavement, attending meetings and conferences, and following proper business protocol. (Baldridge's book on *Executive Manners* even has a chapter on "The Important Business of the Nonprofit World and the Duties of the Nonprofit Board.")

Find your points of reference. Where does your association fit into the world of the other (501) trade, professional, and philanthropic groups?

Because businesses form their base of members, trade associations typically have executives that exercise open, public leadership and make more top-level decisions on their own. Trade groups routinely set standards for the industry they represent, and their board members often have differing educational backgrounds.

In contrast, professional societies or associations often expect their executives to exhibit a quieter leadership style and to execute decisions by preparing information and plans that enable the members to take the lead. Professional associations are composed of individual members, who usually have similar backgrounds and tend to take more of a personal interest in the operations of their association.

Join ASAE. The American Society of Association Executives (ASAE) provides a wealth of information concerning every facet of association work and is the professional association for association executives and director-level staff members. Joining this international group reflects your professional commitment to staying current. Plus, it will deter executive burnout by providing an outlet for your professional growth and learning.

Consider asking your association to provide your ASAE membership as a professional development benefit. And don't overlook the allied society of association executives in your state or region. These local or regional groups often have powerful peer networks, mentoring programs, and other useful resources.

Your Many Roles

As an association executive, you need to be organized and on top of every situation, be it legislative or a member-driven request. You need to live within your budget and plan activities to stimulate member interest and growth. If you have staff added to this mix, personnel activities and organizational operations will complicate the scenario. And your job also entails being an educator—educating your members, the government, and the public. As the face of the association, you must take the leadership role in training, communications, political action, and research.

Did you realize that you would also be a salesperson, ready to sell ideas to the members and staff and to sell the association's mission to the public and legislature? And as the HR person, you are expected to be well-versed in human relationships and interpersonal relations.

And don't forget you're also the accountant, so you need to follow your operational budget and understand the many facets of your association's financial operations and investments.

No matter what the challenge, you'll be able to meet it by applying your administrative and organizational talents—and this book will help you do that. It's a basic compilation of necessities for acculturation into the association nonprofit realm as a new hire. Many other books are far more comprehensive and detailed as to best practices in association financial management, legal and regulatory affairs, and management processes. This primer should be the beginning of many association management books that you add to your personal library.

Good luck on your career path, and enjoy the journey. Together we will advance, promote, and enhance professional association management.

Board-Staff-Volunteer Relationships

By Trudy Aron, CAE

THE RELATIONSHIP BETWEEN THE governing body (hereafter called *board*) and the chief staff executive (hereafter called *CSE*) is a partnership, built on mutual trust, that allows the association to fulfill its mission. In many associations the responsibilities of the board and of the CSE (and any other staff) are blurry. Yet the clearer the responsibilities, the easier it is for each group to perform its respective jobs.

In associations, unlike for-profit businesses, the board decides *what*, but the CSE decides *how*. The CSE works independently from the board but answers to the board. When things are going well, being an association executive is like having your own business without having your personal fortune at stake. When things are not going well, however, it is a very lonely job.

Who Does What

Typically, the board:

- Sets the association's mission and direction.
- Develops policies and strategies for the association.
- Makes decisions that affect the programs and services offered to the association's members.
- Speaks for the association.
- Hires the CSE.

Typically, the CSE:

- Handles the administration of the association (accounting, taxes, office management, and so forth).

- Carries out the directives of the board by turning the policies, programs, and services defined by the board into reality (for example, develops a newsletter, provides education opportunities for members, interacts with other associations, monitors the work of committees).
- Hires and manages association staff.

As the CSE, do you have a detailed job description? If so, do you fully understand your responsibilities? Usually they are either not detailed enough or they are so long as to be daunting. Read them over carefully. They should answer such questions as:

- Who speaks for the association—you or the elected president? If it's you, are there any exceptions?
- Who represents the association at meetings with other associations, legislators, and regulators?
- Are you authorized to sign checks?
- What types of spending controls does the association have? Does anyone other than the board have the authority to obligate the association?

If you aren't sure what your authority is, or if you were hired without a detailed job description, sit down with the elected president and officers and candidly discuss what they expect of you. This discussion benefits both you and the volunteer leaders by enabling all of you to mutually agree on your role. Plus, it helps establish the trusting partnership that is needed to accomplish the association's goals.

Know Your Leaders

Get to know your top elected leaders (president, vice president, secretary, and treasurer.) Typically, these people have served on the board for some time and are knowledgeable about the association's culture. Don't be shy about asking them questions. Check in with the president often—once a week is ideal, especially at first.

Between meetings, communicate often with the entire board; you might, for example, send a weekly e-mail update to let them know of any important developments. Also remember these guidelines:

- No surprises! Be the first to deliver bad news. Don't let your board be caught unaware.
- Don't promise something you can't deliver.

- Never divulge privileged or sensitive information. Although you may have to report something about a member to the board, protect the person's identity.
- At all times, deal ethically with the board.
- Remember to take your direction from the board as a whole, not from individual members (unless authorized by the board).
- Ensure the board funnels all assignments through you, rather than going directly to staff.

The best aspect of association work is that the leaders usually change annually. Of course, the worst aspect of association work is that the leaders usually change annually. When you have good leaders whose terms are ending, find a way for them to continue being active players in the association.

The Role of Volunteers

The smaller the association (or its staff) the greater role the volunteers must play. While the culture of the association plays a big part in the specific roles of each, the work of the small association could never be completed without a staff-volunteer partnership. Here are some tips on working with volunteers:

- Remember that association work often has a low priority for volunteers, no matter how dedicated they are.
- Make sure they understand their responsibility or goal, what resources they have, and when it is due. Remind them of the deadline several times, preferably with humor (for example, send a reminder e-mail showing a target or a finger with a string tied around it).
- Say thanks. Better yet, send a little note to let them know you appreciate the time they devote to the association. Mention their work in your member communications.

Finding a Balance

The magnitude of your CSE responsibilities may seem overwhelming at times. To maintain your sanity,

- Set priorities—but remain flexible. The president or board can help you initially, but ultimately you have to decide what to tackle first.

Your days will often be interrupted by something that cannot wait. This then becomes your first priority.

- Set realistic deadlines for accomplishing tasks. Always plan on a task taking at least twice as long as you think it will.

- Learn to delegate—to staff as well as to volunteers.

- When you simply have to get things done: Shut your door, turn on the answering machine, and don't open your e-mail.

- Find a mentor. The ASAE Small Staff Advisory Committee is a group of CSEs who manage small associations; this committee can provide you with another small association executive who is willing to be a mentor. If you belong to your local society of association executives, make time to attend the meetings and let your colleagues know you are new and could use their advice and assistance.

Contracts

By Robert E. McLean, CAE

E VERY EXECUTIVE DIRECTOR, REGARDLESS of the size of the association, will negotiate and sign a variety of contracts. Some contracts are straightforward and routine. Others can be complex and may require the assistance of legal counsel prior to completion.

Governance Documents

Typically, a newly hired association executive director inherits several association documents that are essentially contracts. Those documents include:

Articles of incorporation. When formed, an association must draft and file articles of incorporation. In some states, these articles will lead to the creation of a certificate of incorporation—a document that serves as a contract between the association and the state.

The articles—which include basic information such as the association's name, address, and officers—create a legally recognized corporation. They explain the nature of the association's structure, its reason for existence, and the activities it will pursue. They also reference the general plans for governance, the individuals or entities the association will serve, the geographic area served, membership requirements, and the type of organization to be created (for-profit corporation; nonprofit corporation; philanthropic, professional, or trade association).

Because these requirements can be quite specific and unique, depending on the jurisdiction involved, most associations seek the help of legal counsel when developing the articles of incorporation. The association retains these permanent documents in perpetuity; they may be filed with the secretary of state's office in the state where your association is located.

Bylaws. Bylaws are a contract between an association and its members. They describe the organizational structure of the board and its officers, membership categories, membership requirements, voting procedures, and other essential guidelines for operating the organization.

Typically, a state requires the submission of bylaws with the application for incorporation. Legal counsel is often necessary when drafting or amending bylaws. Amended bylaws should always be dated, with the date placed at the end of the document. Prior amend dates should remain listed and not deleted, as every date should be documented proof of a bylaw change.

Policy and Procedures Manual. Good association bylaws are concise—only as long as is necessary to include essential, legally mandated information. The details for operating the association are often outlined in a separate document, usually called the policies and procedures manual. Although developed for internal use only and not legally mandated, this document is an extension of the bylaws in that it answers essential questions about how the association manages its day-to-day activities.

This manual varies greatly from one group to another, depending on the type of association involved, its size, its legal structure, and the scope of its activities. The executive director frequently develops the document, which requires board (but not membership) approval. This manual includes detailed explanations of policies (including, perhaps, their origin) and procedures (including consultants and vendors that typically carry out association business).

The policies and procedures manual can be invaluable for smaller associations—especially for one with a newly hired executive director or newly elected board members. That's because the manual answers many of the questions regarding basic operational tasks, ranging from hours of operation to staff responsibilities to investment decisions.

A typical manual covers the following topics:

- Financial management.
- Database management.
- Communication management (including response times for membership communication).

- Board and membership committees (typically including member selection, structure, operational procedures).
- Employee performance standards and appraisals.
- Meeting planning and management processes.
- Membership services.
- Public relations.
- Advocacy.
- Antitrust.

Office Leases

Most associations operate in facilities owned by another organization or individual, typically leased for several years at a time. The search for association offices may be done by staff or with the assistance of a board or ad hoc membership committee. The contracts for office space are prepared for signature by an association board officer or the executive director.

Office leases vary based on the type of facility involved and the scope of services offered by the building management. The resulting document must include certain provisions, based on local and state laws, and should include other provisions for the association's benefit. Negotiating a real estate contract, whether for purchase or lease of office space, requires skills few association executives possess and are best prepared with the help of legal and real estate professionals.

The contract should address issues such as:

- Payment processes and dates.
- Deposits.
- Accessibility (at night, on weekends, and on holidays).
- Routine maintenance.
- Security.
- Capital improvements and repairs.
- Insurance.
- Utilities.
- Renewals.
- Move-in regulations.
- Restrictions on use and subleases.
- Heating and air conditioning (hours of operation, seasonal changes).
- Termination.

Employment Contracts

Negotiating formal contracts for the association's executive director (and sometimes senior staff) can be time consuming and expensive, but doing so provides the advantages of clarifying responsibilities and liability and ensuring a long-term relationship.

Such contracts generally specify the duration of service, responsibilities, the reporting relationship, the performance review process, compensation (pay, benefits, and incentive pay options), termination provisions, and severance pay.

The termination section is frequently the most detailed part of an employment contract and varies depending on employment law in the city or state where the association headquarters reside. Board members are most often concerned with a clear definition of when an employee may be terminated "with cause." The employee is often concerned with any allowance for termination "without cause."

Regardless of the termination circumstances, an effective employment contract addresses issues following termination or resignation. They range from the handling of physical property (office keys and equipment) to intellectual property created by the executive while serving as an association employee. Such clauses typically state that all work created during employment is owned by the association and must be surrendered by the employee upon termination or resignation.

Typically, the association board and employee retain separate legal counsel to draft or review proposed contract language. As an association executive, remember that an employment agreement—like any other contract—is negotiable. Rarely do both parties sign the first draft submitted by either side. Changes are expected, and trade-offs in the benefits area are likely to occur in most negotiations. (If negotiations become contentious, you might enlist the assistance of a third-party mediator.)

Hotel Contracts

Most associations sign at least one contract annually to host a board, committee, or annual meeting. Hotel contracts vary depending on whether the facility is hosting a single-room event or a convention with multiple breakouts and whether additional services will be required (such as audiovisual equipment and food and beverage).

A typical hotel contract includes the following key provisions:

- Number of housing rooms or suites needed, typically listed as room nights (the number of rooms times the number of nights occupied).
- Cut-off dates (the last date by which the association's members may register at the preferred rate).
- Dishonored reservations (how the hotel will respond if it overbooks the hotel and refuses to honor your members' reservations).
- Complimentary guest rooms (typically one free room for every 50 room nights).
- Meeting space (rooms used for the meeting, including when they become accessible and when the association must vacate them).
- Room set-up charges (usually waived if food is purchased during the function).
- Exhibition space (where the association may hold a trade show, including any special requirements such as the use of union labor to set up booths).
- Audiovisual equipment (may be price bundled if using several microphones, screens, and so forth).
- Any surcharges added if you bring in your own audiovisual equipment (computer projector, slide projector, overhead projector, or screens).
- Food and beverage charges (sometimes handled as a separate contract).
- Meal guarantees (the date by which the association must indicate how many meals it needs for a function).
- Payment (due date and acceptable forms of payment).
- Attrition fees (a penalty the association pays if it fails to generate the minimum number of room nights listed in the contract).
- Insurance.
- Cancellation (the last date by which the association can cancel without penalty and the fees due if the association cancels the event after that date).

With the advent of Internet-based travel services, such as Travelocity and Orbitz, and the growing interest in frequent flyer/traveler programs, many associations are finding it difficult to keep their members in the designated host hotel. Association members may prefer to stay at a less expensive hotel or at one where they receive points toward free lodging. As a result, associations often fail to meet the agreed-upon room block and become liable for thousands of dollars in attrition fees.

Once rare, attrition fees are now routine in hotel contracts and can be financially devastating for associations. Conversely, an association that underestimates its room block could see dozens of members turned away from a conference hotel or forced to pay substantially higher rates. As a result, many associations rely on professional meeting planners to handle the details of a conference or convention.

Another standard item in hotel contracts is the "force majeure" clause. It addresses the financial obligations of the hotel and association in the event of a natural and unavoidable catastrophe that prevents or impedes attendance at a contractual event. For example, the clause often references natural disasters—such as floods, earthquakes, and hurricanes—or special circumstances, such as employee strikes or war.

A force majeure clause typically releases an association from any financial obligation if a meeting must be cancelled or when the association's members find it difficult or impossible to attend the meeting. Since September 11, 2001, force majeure clauses have been given greater scrutiny because of concern over acts of terrorism. Terrorism may not be considered, in the legal sense, an act of war. Defining an act of terrorism can be a contentious process. Clarification with the hotel is advisable if this is a major concern for your association's function.

Remember that virtually every aspect of a hotel contract is negotiable. Keep these points in mind before signing a hotel contract:

- Never accept the first offer.
- Consider signing a multi-year contract with a single hotel or hotel chain. Such an agreement ensures greater flexibility on every issue, from room rates to attrition penalties, to cancellation options in the event of terrorism, to parking fees.
- Ask the hotel about special charges.
- Ask how the hotel will respond to any overbooking and what it would do if the event generates higher than anticipated attendance. (For example, can the hotel help the association negotiate a compatible rate at another nearby property?)

In times of economic and political uncertainty, even the best-negotiated hotel contracts cannot preclude the possibility of a poor turnout or a last-minute cancellation. Planning for such a contingency in the association's budget is imperative. (See the chapters titled "Insurance Considerations" and "Meeting Planning Basics" for more information.)

Consultant Contracts

Associations may contract with consultants for outside work. Such projects can range from graphic designers to writers to association management companies and consultants. Depending on the size of the project and its budget—and the association executive's familiarity with the vendor or consultant—such work may only require a simple letter of agreement, rather than a detailed contract requiring a formal review by the association's attorney.

No matter what the size of the project, ensure the association owns the resulting product by addressing the issue of intellectual property in all proposals, letters of agreement, and formal contracts.

Intellectual property can include the association's name, logo, and membership mailing lists. Proprietary information belongs exclusively to the association. For work created outside the association, which can include that done by software developers and lobbyists, the association must have a signed document indicating that it has ownership rights to all intellectual property created by the contractor.

The association's legal counsel can draft standard language addressing ownership of all intellectual property.

Finance for Small Associations

By Sharon K. Mellor, CAE

S OUND FINANCIAL MANAGEMENT IS critical in all associations, but particularly in small ones. Lean budgets mean that you must operate the organization efficiently to provide members with good value for their dues dollars.

As the head of a small association, you may not have a staff person to handle the accounting and finance functions. Therefore, as executive director, your responsibilities include keeping financial records, preparing accurate financial statements, budgeting, safeguarding and managing the organization's assets, and complying with federal and state reporting requirements.

In most cases, you will have an elected treasurer and perhaps a finance or investment committee of the board to provide oversight and input. Ultimately, you report on the financial activities of your association to the board of directors.

Budgeting

The association budget typically is prepared for a 12-month period. This time period—or fiscal year—may coincide with the calendar year (January 1 through December 31) or may begin and end at any other time of the year (for example, July 1 through June 30).

Careful budgeting is a key to sound financial management. Budget preparation helps you and your leaders think through the association's products and services and their corresponding costs. The process assists you in identifying priorities and focusing on key activities. In addition, your budget serves as a tool against which your actual income and expenses may be compared on a continuous basis. This comparison allows you to spot trends and make corrections early in the game.

Remember that the budget is written on paper, not carved in stone. The scenarios you anticipated when creating the budget may not materialize, so make it flexible enough to shift resources as necessary.

Types of Budgets. An association's *operating budget* details income and expense expectations for all of its functions, such as administration, governance, membership, meetings and conventions, and publications. The *cash budget,* which is developed from the operating budget, indicates when expected revenue will be received and when expected expenditures will be made.

This information, along with projections regarding earnings from investments, allows you to estimate cash flow to ensure that cash is available to meet your association's obligations. It also identifies those times when surplus cash may be available for investment.

The *capital budget* is used for planning the purchase of, or improvements to, such assets as the association office or equipment. Capital expenditures are not included as part of the operating budget because they affect the association's functions for many years. Only the depreciation of capital assets is included in the operating budget.

Preparing an operating budget. Some association executives believe they can easily create a budget for a new fiscal period by taking the current year's budget and adding a percentage for change to each line item. This strategy, however, can carry over misjudgments from year to year.

Other executives assume that every project will pay for itself. First, they estimate expenses and then assume they will generate income to cover those expenses. This is treading on dangerous ground. If their only goal is to prepare a balanced budget, these executives may underestimate or completely overlook the possibilities of declining income.

Perhaps the best approach to developing your budget is to first make a realistic estimate of income for the year, then build the expense budget. First, identify the activities your organization expects to carry out during the budget year. Then estimate the revenues that each program or function will realistically generate. Income categories might include membership dues, meeting registrations, sponsorships, exhibit fees, charitable contributions, and investment income.

Next, estimate the costs of carrying out those services. In addition to direct costs (such as printing, postage, and meeting room costs) the budget must include indirect costs (such as space, staff salaries, and utilities). Some budgets are constructed so that direct expenses and income are shown for each individual function or project while all indirect costs are shown under a general heading (such as "administration"). Other budgets are constructed so that a portion of indirect expenses are charged against each project or function.

Some association executives believe this second method provides them with the "true cost" of an activity. To prepare a budget of this type, you would need to estimate the percentage of time during the year that each staff member would spend on a particular project, for example, then allocate this percentage of the total salary to the project.

Don't be discouraged if your first attempt at the budget shows that your estimated expenses exceed your estimated revenues. This simply means you must sharpen your editing pencil and look for ways to trim costs. You'll either have to scale back projects or look for less expensive means of achieving your objectives.

Once you have achieved a balance between revenues and costs, submit the budget to the association's elected leaders for approval. The budget typically is presented as a comparison to budgeted and actual revenues and expenses for the previous fiscal year. Current fiscal year revenues and expenditures to date are also an important part of the overall budget package.

To help you track revenues and expenditures, hundreds of accounting software packages are available. Because these products provide a varying mix of features and capabilities, think through your requirements before making a choice. Define the types of reports you will need to generate, consider the types of transactions you must process, think about any required interfaces with other software products (for example, with membership database software), and determine the level of security necessary for the financial information. Consider your budget, but base your final decision on value to your organization as well as on price.

Financial Reports

Financial records for associations typically are prepared using accrual, rather than cash, accounting. This means that transactions are recorded in the period when the program activity occurs, not when the financial activity occurs.

Accrual accounting provides financial reports that link the income and expense from a particular activity. For example, the registration income and meeting space fees for a convention would be recorded in the period during which the meeting took place, rather than in the period during which the registration fees were received or when the meeting space bills were paid. In this way, both you and the volunteer leaders can easily tell how profitable the event was.

Association financial reports should be timely, accurate, comprehensive, and clear. A good test of the clarity of your financial statements is if, after reading them, a non-accountant would have a good understanding of your organization's overall financial activities.

There are three common types of financial reports. The Statement of Financial Position (*balance sheet*) lists association assets (cash, office equipment, and others) and association liabilities (salaries payable or outstanding invoices). The difference between association assets and association liabilities is its equity. One balance sheet is prepared at the beginning of the fiscal period and one at the end for comparison purposes.

The Statement of Activity (*income statement*) shows the activities of the association and describes the changes in net assets over the fiscal period. The Statement of Change in Financial Position (*cash flow statement*) describes the change in cash over the fiscal period.

These reports are useful for identifying and understanding trends over time, so they typically are presented for the two previous years.

Financial Controls

The basis for any sound internal control system is the segregation of duties. Ideally, no one individual should control all aspects of any transaction: initiation (receipt of a dues payment check), authorization (verification of the payment against the dues invoice), asset custody (preparing the check for bank deposit), recording (entry into the financial record), and verification (reconciliation of the bank statement).

Internal controls are especially difficult in small associations, where the number of staff members is not large enough for distribution of financial responsibilities. To provide internal control in an association with only one staff member, a volunteer leader—perhaps the treasurer—should be responsible for some of these duties.

The role of an *external auditor* is to verify the information contained in your association's financial reports and issue an opinion as to whether the reports conform to generally accepted accounting principles. The external auditor also will assess your risk and issue recommendations to minimize it. The audit report may contain footnotes or other explanatory information that will aid readers in understanding the report.

The auditor will not examine each and every financial transaction. Instead, he or she will look at a representative sample. The tighter your internal controls and procedures, the smaller the number of transactions the auditor will need to examine.

An external audit will provide several benefits. They include enhanced credibility of your financial statements, professional assistance in developing statements and procedures, advice on internal controls, and assistance in tax reporting and compliance requirements.

To select an audit firm, send a request for proposal with basic information about the association's finances. Most associations select firms that have similar nonprofit clients and are therefore familiar with applicable accounting standards. Other factors to consider are reputation, fees, continuity of staff, and ability to respond quickly to your needs.

The proposals you receive will include a project fee, which is based on the estimated hours for completing the audit. You can keep the fees lower by ensuring that adequate internal controls and verification procedures are in place. Also, a pre-audit meeting can streamline the process if you ask the auditor what information he or she will need to access and how it should be presented.

Some associations prefer to develop long-term relationships with auditors, using the same firm each year. Over time, the auditors come to understand the association processes and records, helping the audit go more smoothly and quickly. Other associations find value in changing auditors every three to five years. An audit firm approaching the books with a fresh eye may offer valuable recommendations. Too, the association enhances the credibility of the audit by eliminating the possibility that the audit firm has become too familiar and "chummy" with the organization.

Safeguarding Your Financial Position

Wise association leaders set aside *operating reserves*—funds to use as a cushion in times of financial stress. But how much is enough?

There is no hard and fast rule regarding appropriate levels of reserves. Typically, however, the smaller the association budget, the larger the percentage of the annual budget that should be set aside in a reserve fund. This is because organizations with small budgets have less flexibility in trimming costs during times of financial hardship.

According to the ASAE *Operating Ratio Report,* 12th edition, more than half of associations with a formal reserve policy define their reserves as the organization's net unrestricted assets and have a median target of 50 percent of the annual operating budget. Other associations more narrowly define operating reserves as liquid assets (cash and investments that can be quickly converted to cash) and have a median reserve target of 33 percent of the operating budget.

Your board of directors should set a policy regarding its definition of operating reserves and the level of reserves appropriate for the association. Strive to reach that goal and maintain reserves at that level. Achieving the operating reserve goal will ensure your organization's current and future financial health while maintaining its ability to meet critical member needs.

Many associations invest these reserve funds conservatively in CDs and fixed income accounts. Your association's investment policy should cover the operating reserve fund and detail permissible investments, taking into account the organization's risk profile. Your association also should pay attention to the liquidity of the operating reserve funds and define parameters for short-term and long-term opportunities.

Aim for a mix of funding sources, so all of your association eggs are not in one basket. Pay careful attention to trends within your various sources of funding: dues, exhibit sales, advertising, grants, product sales, meeting registrations, investment income, sponsorships, donations, and so forth. Be prepared to act if a particular source of revenue appears to be faltering.

Trend-watching is especially important in organizations that depend heavily on one source of revenue. According to ASAE's *Operating Ratio Report,* the smaller the association and staff size, the more it relies on dues income as its major source of revenue. If your association fits into this category, carefully track trends in your membership categories and look for ways to diversify your sources of income. To compensate for declining revenue in one area, you may consider such strategies as cutting expenses, promoting existing products and services to new markets, or developing new products and services.

Also review your current offerings to ensure you are maximizing their value. For example, perhaps you are not realizing the income you should from your educational conference. If you determine, by consulting outside sources, that the market value of your conference offerings is higher than you had thought, you might consider increasing registration fees.

Investments

If the total money your association has available for investment is relatively small, you may find that a no-load mutual fund or a common stock fund is a good investment. These funds provide a convenient and low-cost form of investment management. With so many mutual funds to choose from, each having different investment goals and varying degrees of risk, shop around to see which suits your situation best.

If your organization has a larger amount of money to invest, consider seeking professional advice on your portfolio. You may retain a professional to simply provide advice or to recommend and handle the actual buying and selling of investments.

Your board, or a subgroup of the board such as a finance or investment committee, should develop an *investment policy* for approval by the governing body. This investment road map should indicate percentage ranges for investment classes such as fixed income, cash and equivalents, and equities. The policy should address acceptable and unacceptable investments (for example, corporate junk bonds), limits on stock purchases of any specific company, minimum ratings for bonds, and other criteria of importance to your organization. The policy should also address the frequency on which the portfolio should be rebalanced.

Taxing Issues

Don't think that because your association is tax-exempt, you do not need to worry about tax management. In fact, your organization is subject to many regulations, including Unrelated Business Income Tax (UBIT) rules and exempt-status preservation rules, and must comply with various federal and state reporting requirements.

Because the laws, forms, and filing requirements can be complicated, you might want to enlist the services of a tax professional to prepare your returns. Your external audit firm may be willing to do this for an additional fee.

If an IRS controversy arises, you may be asked to provide documentation. Make sure you have policies and procedures for retaining such documents as board minutes, signed contracts, letters of understanding, correspondence, copies of checks, and tax returns.

All not-for-profit organizations exempt from income tax must file federal *Form 990* if their annual gross receipts are normally more than $25,000. Nonprofits with gross receipts of $25,000 or less are not required to file. (Form 990-EZ can be used if the organization's total assets are less than $250,000 and the organization's gross receipts are less than $100,000.) These forms must be filed by the 15th day of the 5th month following the close of the calendar or fiscal year; a penalty of $10 per day is assessed for filing late.

The organization must file Form 990-T if it has unrelated business income or is calculating Proxy Tax—a tax levied on lobbying expenses up to total dues revenue for the year, which requires multiplying the total lobbying expenditures by the applicable tax rate.

Virtually every association is subject to corporate taxes on its unrelated business income, or income from products and services outside the organization's tax-exempt purpose. (The information below is intended to provide general information, not legal advice; because regulations change, seek the assistance of your tax professional.)

Pay particular attention to these areas:

Royalty fees, such as those from insurance programs or credit cards your association endorses, are exempt from UBIT. To avoid labeling non-qualifying income as royalties, clarify your interpretation of the royalty exclusion.

Trade show exhibit income is usually tax-exempt if your show is educational in nature and includes a cross-section of industry products.

Be sure to understand the rules as they apply to your association's trade show.

Volunteer-run activities in 501(c)(3) organizations are tax exempt. If you are directing a charitable organization, be sure you understand this exemption.

Advertising in the association's publication is typically subject to UBIT.

Lobbying activity also has tax implications; 501(c)(3) organizations are exempt because they do not engage in lobbying.

For 501(c)(6) organizations that incur lobbying expenses related to federal and state legislation, you must calculate the percentage of dues not deductible by a member for income tax purposes. Divide the total amount of lobbying expenditures incurred by total dues revenues: Lobbying Expenses ÷ Dues Revenue = Disallowable Percentage.

The association must report the nondeductible portion of membership dues directly to the member. For example, you might include a statement such as this on a membership application: *The tax deductibility of dues paid to XYZ Association as an ordinary and necessary business expense is subject to restrictions imposed as a result of lobbying activities. XYZ Association estimates that the nondeductible portion of your annual dues is _____%.*

For renewing members, provide a reasonable estimate of the percentage of their dues payment that will be nondeductible for the coming year. For example: *As a result of XYZ Association's lobbying activities, the percentage of dues that may be deducted as an ordinary and necessary business expense is subject to restriction. XYZ Association estimates the nondeductible percentage of your dues payment to be ___%.*

The membership forms of nonprofits are also required to include the following statement: *Dues are not deductible as charitable contributions for income tax purposes. Dues may be considered ordinary and necessary business deductions.* This statement corrects the general public's misunderstanding that dues are deductible as charitable contributions. Only contributions made to 501(c)(3) organizations are deductible.

Communicating with the Board

As executive director, regularly apprise the board of your organization's financial status. Especially if unexpected financial losses occur, you must inform the board, honestly and directly, of the extent of the variance. In a shortfall situation, present not only the bad news and its effect on your operations but also one or more means of addressing the problem.

Insurance Considerations

By Kim B. Stoneking, CAE

G IVEN OUR LITIGIOUS SOCIETY, be aware of the basic forms of insurance coverage for professional and trade associations. If you are new to your association, check with your predecessor, treasurer, bookkeeper, or accountant regarding the types of coverage already in force.

Risk management is the process of identifying the risks that could threaten your association. You and the board of directors should determine those risks important to insure against and decide how much the association can afford in the event of a loss.

A trustworthy insurance professional will ensure the coverage lines up with your insurance goals and your level of risks. Depending on your level of risk, for example, you may wish to keep deductibles low and purchase as much insurance coverage as the association can afford.

The following is not an exhaustive list of the insurance coverage available to an association. Discuss with a licensed insurance professional the types and amount of coverage your specific association needs.

Directors and Officers Liability (D&O)

The purpose of this coverage is to insure against wrongful acts by your elected volunteer leaders, such as mismanagement of funds, discrimination, or other related employment actions; it usually covers payment of damages and costs of defense. This coverage is for liability on the part of the organization's officers and directors when acting on behalf of the association; do not confuse this coverage with professional liability coverage.

Even though your organization's level of risk and claims history is probably low, you should not be without this type of insurance. Short of proving bad faith or fraud, success on a claim of this type is remote, but defending them can be very expensive.

This type of insurance coverage is becoming increasingly difficult to find and can be quite complicated. The coverage, terms, exclusions, conditions limitations, and endorsements can vary greatly depending on the carrier, so analyze several policies.

Event Cancellation

Insurance is available to cover expenses and lost revenue resulting from cancellation of meetings. While associations have long been insuring against meeting losses resulting from such calamities as power outage, a strike, or a roof collapse, this form of insurance has gone through tremendous turmoil since September 11, 2001. Cost of this coverage has risen, and terms are more restricted.

Operating meetings without this form of coverage will depend on your level of risk and potential loss. An association can take several small steps to control risk, such as revising cancellation provisions for meeting attendees and revising the criteria for canceling meetings.

Employee Dishonesty (Bonding)

Coverage is available for losses arising from employee embezzlement or theft. Highly recommended for all organizations, this coverage is relatively inexpensive when compared to the potential loss. Its cost will likely vary depending on the amount and types of funds flowing through the association. Association officers who have monetary responsibility may also be covered by bonding.

Errors and Omissions (E&O)

If your association is involved in setting standards or has an accreditation program, this may be necessary coverage. This coverage defends against such claims as allegations of dangerous standards or having unqualified accreditation recipients. Also consider this coverage if your association is involved in extensive educational opportunities for members.

Meeting Planning Basics

By Dana Saal, CAE

AN ASSOCIATION'S MEETINGS ARE frequently its bloodline and its glue. Meetings infuse much-needed cash and make up a large portion of the budget—sometimes most of it. Meetings create opportunities for members to gather and remind them why they belong to the association. To some members, your meetings *are* the association.

For these reasons, carefully planned events are essential. For the first-time planner, the process can be daunting—especially if you're holding other titles such as executive director or membership director. The key is to have a plan, know what comes next, and use your resources wisely so you don't have to do it all by yourself.

Before you start planning, however, clarify why the meeting exists. Even if it's your association's 79th annual convention or your 10th committee meeting, you need to be able to state the meeting's purpose. In other words: What do you want to accomplish by having the meeting or event? Is it for educational, planning, or social purposes—or a combination of these?

Your objective, for example, might be to make a decision, to communicate a message, to plan, to train or retrain, to network, or to have fun. (Making money can even be an objective, but it should be in combination with objectives that benefit the attendees.) Then customize the meeting's objective by completing one of these sentences:

"After this meeting, participants should be able to..."

"The theme of this meeting is _____ and I want to accomplish _____."

Make the objectives measurable by using numbers, time lines, or skill sets. Communicate them in advance to all meeting participants by including a list in the registration materials. And don't forget to use the objective as you plan the meeting: Refer to it again and again as you make decisions.

Another way to define your meeting is by defining your audience. At times, you will define your audience before your objective, and vice versa. The key is to know who you are targeting so you can customize many aspects of your event including topic selection, publicity, and even registration fees.

To know how and what to plan for your audience, assess their needs through either formal or informal surveys. You might, for example, simply ask members to define their current challenges. Keep in mind the timing of the event. If your convention is 12 months away, consider what their needs will be at that time.

Types of Meetings

You will plan many *one-day meetings* in your life as an association executive. They will be for educational seminars, retreats, and board and committee meetings. One-day meetings are typically scheduled to make decisions and plan (board or committee meetings) or to share information (educational seminars).

As you look at your calendar and see that it's time for another committee meeting, be sure you have a reason to meet. Members will appreciate your canceling a non-substantive meeting more than they will appreciate your holding a meeting just because it's the third Thursday of the month. Similarly, don't schedule an educational seminar that will not benefit the audience. Attendees deserve meaty information in exchange for their time and money.

Multi-day meetings include in-depth educational seminars and conventions. Seminars will be singularly focused, while a convention will have many facets.

Associations frequently host a *trade show* in conjunction with their conventions. Trade shows, or exhibits, gather industry suppliers in one space to increase company awareness or sales. The show provides another non-dues source of income for the organization through sales of table-top exhibits or exhibit booths. Table-top exhibits are typically for smaller shows and are more informal. They consist of 6' or 8' draped (with a tablecloth) tables that are typically set up on the perimeter of a ballroom. The venue provides the tables, cloths, and one or two chairs.

The association pays the venue a fee for each table set up. Ask to be charged a flat fee for set-up rather than a daily rate.

Exhibit booths are for medium to large shows or for exhibitors with large displays. They consist of floor space that is defined on three sides by pipe and drape (metal pipe with curtains) that are provided by a show decorator. Back drapes are 8' high and usually include a one-line sign with the exhibitor's company name. Side drapes are 3' high. Floor space is typically 8×8', 8×10', or 10×10'. Larger displays use (and pay for) multiple booth spaces.

A show decorator sets up and tears down the booths. Each booth is set with the equipment for which you contract and can include the company sign, table(s) draped to match show colors, chairs, and carpeting. The decorator will charge a flat fee per booth for the entire event. The decorator can also provide other equipment for both your exhibitors and your on-site needs, such as registration desks and chairs.

Show decorators also provide drayage—accepting cargo from exhibitors and delivering it to their booth space. Exhibitors contract directly with the show decorator for this service, which also includes shipping to the cargo's next destination. The show decorator will send an exhibit packet to each exhibitor several weeks before your show; ask for a sample kit when you hire the decorator. Some show decorators also have order forms online. They send a letter to each exhibitor with the Web site information and a password for your show.

Meeting Timing

Timing can affect your meeting's success. The wrong pattern (days of the week—for example, a Monday-Wednesday pattern) or the wrong month can impact your attendee or exhibitor registration and, therefore, your budget.

As you consider the month of your event, keep in mind:

- Weather for the meeting location as well as the starting point for the attendees. (Pleasant weather in Florida doesn't matter if the Northeast could be buried in two feet of snow.)

- Industry conflicts. (Farmers can't meet during harvest; accountants can't meet in March.)

- Venue cost. (Each geographical area has seasons—peak, shoulder, and off—and room costs change with each season. Peak will be the most expensive; off-season, the least.)

As you consider the pattern of your event, keep in mind:

- Busy days for your attendees. (Many businesses find it difficult to be out of the office on Mondays and Fridays.)
- Venue cost. (Some hotels will charge less if your pattern fits into their busy/idle pattern.)
- Transportation. (If flying is involved, flights are cheapest for Saturday and between Monday noon and Thursday noon. Sunday is considered a peak day.)

Selecting a Venue

Use your objectives and audience definition to decide where you want to meet and what kind of facility you want to use. If your list of options is national, the task can be daunting. To narrow your choices, poll your colleagues in other states for a list of cities in which they have met. You can also ask your members for suggestions.

When you have identified the city, choosing the venue is your next step. A venue that is too expensive, too difficult to reach, or simply a bad fit will discourage registrations for the current event or, worse, for future events. The local convention and visitor's bureau (CVB) or chamber of commerce can provide a list of meeting places that fulfill your criteria. They will also let the venues know that you are interested through a request for proposal (RFP). You provide the CVB with a list of meeting needs (number of sleeping rooms, your agenda, and so forth) and the CVB will send the RFP to all the hotels, which will respond to you directly.

This process enables you to compare properties on the same merits, but it can create a lot of paperwork. Feel free to put parameters on your request that limit responses. You may say, for example, that you want to hear only from hotels that can offer your preferred room rate or that have indoor pools.

You can do an initial screening of many properties by visiting their Web sites. Many Web sites include interior photos, virtual tours, floor plans, and even menus. If you're looking at a chain hotel, be sure to search for the property's own Web site; it will have more information and photos than what's available on the corporate site.

Associations frequently meet in hotels where sleeping rooms, meeting space, audiovisual equipment, and food and beverage are available in one place. Although hotels are common and convenient, don't limit yourself to them if another type of space better fits your budget, objectives, or audience needs.

Banquet halls offer all the services of a hotel except the sleeping rooms. They serve as comfortable sites for one-day meetings. A drawback can be their pricing. Carefully read the contract: Your rental rate may only include space. You would then have to rent tables, chairs, linens, china, and silverware.

In addition, some require you to guarantee the number of attendees when you sign the contract. That means that if you book the space eight months out you are required to give the guarantee (the actual number of people you will pay for) at that time. You could under-guarantee, or give the facility a lower number than you anticipate, but then you run the risk of being assigned space that is too small. Work with the sales representative to ensure that you don't overpay or underestimate your space.

A *conference center* is set up like a hotel (or a banquet hall if it doesn't have sleeping rooms), but provides a complete meeting package (CMP). Conference centers are good choices for either one-day or multi-day events. The center charges a per-person price and will provide the sleeping rooms, meeting space, breaks, meals, and audiovisual equipment. You might find this option expensive, but it is convenient.

A *resort* is a high-end hotel that can offer the perfect place for a long-range planning event or even a small convention. A resort provides a relaxed atmosphere in a pleasant environment where extracurricular activities can be pursued. Your cost can be more than you'll find in a standard hotel, but you're paying for the high-end service and amenities. Resorts are typically located in remote areas, so keep your attendee's travel in mind.

A *university campus* can offer a low-cost alternative to traditional meeting space. If your timing is right, overnight accommodations are inexpensive, food service is available, and there are a variety of learning environments to use. On the other hand, parking can be difficult; the accommodations are typically dorm rooms (think bunk beds) with group bathrooms; and, unless the university has a formal events department, it can be difficult to find help once the meeting gets started. Some universities are courting the association market and have set up departments to service meetings, so don't write off this option entirely.

Also consider *corporate meeting space*. Start by looking at your neighboring association offices. Many have formal meeting space that they are willing to lend or rent out for others' use. Unless the office is well stocked, you would have to contract separately for your audiovisual equipment and catering. Also, note how difficult it is to find the building and park. The last thing you want is attendees who are grumpy because they got lost looking for the meeting site.

The Site Inspection

Once you have narrowed your venue choices, you might want to make a site inspection, or site visit. This may be as informal as running over to the banquet hall for a quick tour or as formal as flying to the city, staying for one or two nights, eating at the various restaurants and bars in the hotel, and touring with the sales manager. Hotel sales managers are used to hosting site inspections and want you to take the time to thoroughly investigate what they have to offer. They know a bad fit will hurt them just as much as it will hurt you.

Each site visit is different, but in addition to the standard meeting and tour, you might be invited to meet the hotel VIPs, receive a thank you gift, or be treated to a nice suite. Site visits can be fun and make you love your job. They are also subjective. The hotel might pay for your expenses to travel to and stay at their property. Ask in advance how expenses will be handled, but you can expect that your room will be covered. Larger hotels might also pay for your meals and airfare. All-in-all, everyone is on his or her best behavior and you are shown the best side of the hotel.

Not surprisingly, ethical issues can come into play. The question is whether the hotel is "buying" your business by treating you specially. The best way to handle site visits is to accept invitations only for venues that you are truly considering. If you think that the hotel is offering you excessive gifts or perks, decline them. Property selection should be based on needs being met, not treats being offered.

If your association can afford it, a mystery visit gives you a look at a property from the eyes of an attendee. You don't tell anyone you're visiting. You make your own reservation for a standard room, you eat in the hotel, you observe from the outside. It's a great way to evaluate the property as an attendee would. Before you leave, be sure to introduce yourself to the sales staff so you know them.

Your primary goals are to get a first-hand look at the facility layout to see if your event will fit and whether the facility is appropriate for your attendees' needs and tastes. You'll want to assess the overall condition of the property, including cleanliness and atmosphere, and determine what kind of meeting support you can expect.

If you have a formal tour with a sales manager, come prepared with your meeting details and history. (What venue did you use last year? What worked? What didn't work?) Have a copy of your meeting agenda on hand as you tour the facility so you can compare your needs to the space. Finally, if your site visit will include meetings outside of the hotel (with other suppliers or venues), let all parties know your schedule in advance so they can accurately plan their time and give you the attention you need.

Contracts

When to book a venue should be based on your association's needs, not on a set formula. If you have an event that uses a lot of meeting space (lots of session rooms and exhibit space) but not a lot of sleeping rooms, it will be more difficult to find space. It is not a great piece of business for the hotel—which makes money on sleeping rooms—so start looking at venues about two years in advance, if possible.

One-day meetings and even smaller conventions can be booked up to the last minute depending on how much time you want to spend looking for the appropriate space. Less lead time will limit availability.

To maximize your planning time and increase your opportunity to book an appropriate venue, start the process about 18 months out. When you are ready to book the venue (sign a contract) you will need to estimate the number of sleeping rooms needed and the attendance at meals. Certainly, it is difficult to estimate these numbers in advance—especially if you're working several months or even years out—so refer to your event history. If the event is new, rely on your gut feeling and member surveys. If it's a repeat event but you don't have a history, start compiling one now. (An Event History Form is available on the CD-ROM accompanying this book.)

Sleeping room rates, space rental, and food and beverage minimums will all be set based on your attendance figures. A lot rides on these elusive numbers; associations have paid thousands of dollars in fees because anticipated (minimum) numbers were not met. Overestimating results in hotel charges, while underestimating could result in inadequate space. Talk with your venue sales manager to settle on a figure that your association can support in either attendance or penalties if you don't meet the minimum.

The key figure for a multi-day event is the number of sleeping rooms your association will be using. The *sleeping room block* consists of a set number of sleeping rooms held by the hotel for use by your attendees for each night of your event. Your event will be expected to *pick up* (use) most of the rooms in the block. If your attendees don't use the rooms, your contract will likely require that the association pay for the unused rooms (*attrition*).

A room block summary for a 155-attendee multi-day event might look like this:

ROOM TYPE	SUN, NOV 6	MON, NOV 7	TUES, NOV 8	WED, NOV 9	TOTALS
Single/King	8	40	32	1	81
Double/Double	10	50	44	2	106
Junior Suite	4	15	12	0	31
Presidential Suite	1	1	1	0	3
Total Rooms	23	106	89	3	221

Typical hotel rooms can be described as follows:
- Single/King (or queen)—one bed for one or two people
- Double/Double—two beds for two, three, or four people
- Junior Suite—varies, but typically is one bed with either extra space or a separate room for a table and formal seating area
- Presidential Suite—same as a Junior Suite but features more space and furniture and can include a dining room table, two bathrooms, and a full kitchen. The rate is usually more than an association can spend on a room and is typically given to the association on a complimentary basis—if you ask.

The contract will also list the charge for each type of room. You will see something like this on your contract:

Single/King $105
Double/Double $115
Junior Suite $135
Presidential Suite . . . . .complimentary

The room block for each night is different because it reflects the arrival pattern of attendees. In the preceding example, a few attendees will arrive Sunday afternoon, perhaps for an early board of directors meeting on Monday morning. The majority will arrive on Monday for the late-morning opening session and stay Tuesday. Most, but not all, will stay for the closing banquet Tuesday night and depart on Wednesday morning. A few will stay an extra night for business or personal reasons.

Your total room block is 221 *room nights*—the total number of rooms for the entire event. Your *peak night* (largest pick-up) is Monday. Room use is counted when attendees make their reservations and indicate that they are with your group. Although each is different, your contract will likely specify that to fulfill your contract, your association will have to use 80 percent, or 168 room nights. If you use 167 or fewer rooms, your association will be charged the difference times the per room cost. So, if you're paying $105 per room and you use only 145 rooms, you will be charged 23 rooms × $105, or $2,415.

Your attendees might go online to book a hotel and find the same room at the same hotel for $97—and they will take it. They do not have loyalty to your room block, just to their pocketbooks. Therefore, you will find that your attendees are in the hotel, but not in the block because they made the reservations online rather than through the hotel reservation department. Or, you'll hear of attendees staying at a hotel two blocks away because they got a $79 rate.

Reduce the possibility of being charged an attrition fee by educating your attendees about room blocks and how they affect the bottom line (in other words, conference registration fees could increase). Offer incentives for them to use the room block, such as a reduced registration fee, complimentary meal tickets, or an upgrade to a suite (standard room rate for a nicer room).

In addition, add a clause to your venue contract that says rooms booked from all sources and at all rates, not just those from the reservation department, should be counted against the block. To ensure you get credit for all association guests staying in the hotel, sit down with your sales manager and cross reference every name on your final registration list. Do this before the event concludes to ensure accuracy on your bill. (Do this with your sales manager rather than the reservation manager because the former also gets credit for every room booked. He or she will want to account for all of your rooms.)

Contracts might also have food and beverage minimums. Based on your projected attendance and planned food functions, the hotel will forecast anticipated revenue and establish a minimum amount the association is required to spend to meet its contract obligations. Say, for example, you are anticipating 155 attendees. You have planned two continental breakfasts (valued at $12 each), one lunch (valued at $17) and two dinners (valued at $25 each). Based on your 155 attendees and possible food income of $91 per person, you F&B (food and beverage) minimum would be $14,105.

As with the room block, your association will be charged the difference if it doesn't meet the F&B minimum. The hotel can calculate how much money you're spending on F&B so ask regularly during the event. If you find that you're not meeting the minimum, simply add more food. You have to spend the money anyway—and your attendees will love seeing an ice cream sundae break in the middle of the afternoon or an open bar at dinner.

In addition to the attrition clauses for room blocks and food and beverage (which are at most big or chain hotels, but not all small properties), read cancellation clauses carefully. Venues have a sliding scale of damages based on when you cancel your event. Canceling simply to change venues will cost you 100 percent in anticipated revenues. Canceling for other reasons is acceptable but can also cost depending on your timing. Here is sample of a sliding scale:

Cancellation Date	Cancellation Penalty
18 to 24 months before 11/6/06	25% of anticipated revenue
12 to 18 months before 11/6/06	50% of anticipated revenue
6 to 12 months before 11/6/06	75% of anticipated revenue
less than 6 months before 11/6/06	100% of anticipated revenue

This method of calculating attrition is inaccurate because specific dollar amounts are not listed. Ask the hotel to list the exact dollar figure charged at each point. A better scale would look like this:

Cancellation Date	Cancellation Penalty
18 to 24 months before 11/6/06	$11,250 (25% of anticipated revenue)
12 to 18 months before 11/6/06	$22,500 (50% of anticipated revenue)
6 to 12 months before 11/6/06	$33,750 (75% of anticipated revenue)
less than 6 months before 11/6/06	$45,000 (100% of anticipated revenue)

In an emergency or for unavoidable situations, hotels might waive cancellation fees if you rebook the event. Nonetheless, a cancellation clause should not be taken lightly. Before signing anything, be confident that your meeting will be held and that your audience base is supportive. The contract has the final say.

You will be faced with several other clauses in your contract. As with any contract, review each clause carefully and know what you're signing. Although the contracting process sounds intimidating and one-sided, many aspects are negotiable. The key is to ask *before* you sign on the dotted line. Some things to negotiate in a hotel contract are listed below. Don't expect to get all of them, so prioritize your list before presenting it to the property.

- Room rate. If you know your attendees will balk at anything over $105, for example, make sure your sales manager knows this and make it a top priority in your negotiating.

- Complimentary rooms. The hotel will offer one comp room for every 50 room nights. For 221 room nights, for example, your association would get four complimentary room nights. You can ask for the threshold to be 45 or 40.

- Upgraded rooms. The hotel will offer the junior suites, the full suites, or the presidential suite at the group's single room rate.

- Parking rates. If the hotel owns the lot, it can provide complimentary tickets to all hotel guests—or even to any attendee, even those not staying overnight.

- Free use of parking space(s) in front of the hotel (especially handy at hotels with decks).

- Free use of (or deeply discounted) audiovisual equipment owned by the hotel. Plan to pay for the technician to support the equipment.

- Concessions on pre-event planning meetings. Let's say you hold your board of directors meeting at the hotel before the event so you can show off the property. (This helps the hotel because it pre-sells the property to potential attendees and can reassure board members who are unsure about your venue selection.) In turn, ask the hotel to provide goods and services that are complimentary or deeply discounted. This could include sleeping rooms, food and beverage, or VIP baskets. Also ask that the sleeping rooms you use for any pre-event meeting count toward your convention room block.

- One complimentary microphone in each meeting room.
- Complimentary coffee or refreshment break.
- Complimentary meal for a VIP meeting, such as a board breakfast.
- Complimentary VIP baskets delivered to key volunteers and speakers.
- Complimentary child or spouse program.

Your contract will also include language about how to set up a *master account* that establishes credit for your association. You may be required to pay an advance deposit, but having a master account allows you to charge all your expenses and then be billed after your event. To set up the account you will be asked to complete a credit application that includes references from other hotels.

Some venues will require proof of liability insurance when you book a meeting. Consult your insurance agent for details. Consider getting *event cancellation insurance*—insurance against unanticipated loss—if your event is the source of a significant percentage of your budget. Cost will be a factor, but the insurance is worthwhile if your dates, location, or even the economy put you at risk for loss. The closer you are to your event date, the more the insurance will cost—so shop early. Some policies rebate a portion of the premium if you don't file a claim.

Developing a Budget and Agenda

As with any project, a well thought-out budget will aid your decision-making process. The key is to include everything—and add a cushion.

Multi-day event costs seem to take on a life of their own. Adding an extra microphone to a meeting room can end up costing an additional $100 on your final bill—$50 for the microphone and $50 for the mixer required to make two or more microphones work in one room. Requesting six more sodas can easily cost $17; another gallon of coffee might run $82.

Use a budget worksheet to identify your income sources (be conservative) and expenses (be generous). When you're done, add another 10 percent to expenses to cover everything you forgot, you didn't anticipate, or was requested by your president at the last minute.

Your event agenda includes more than hiring a keynote speaker and planning a few meals. You also have to consider session topics and scheduling, networking time, and when your attendees will arrive and depart. Your objective should guide you as you create an agenda for any event, whether it's a one-day meeting or multi-day convention.

For a one-day event, include time for breaks and networking, as well as the educational portion. Many professionals will say that their best ideas come from the conversations that happen in between the official events or during meals of association gatherings.

A multi-day event requires the same considerations, on a larger scale. Creating a convention agenda is like piecing together a puzzle that has more than one solution. Start by laying out all your pieces: educational sessions, breaks, meal functions, special events, the awards ceremony, keynote presentations, exhibits, your business meeting, committee meetings, and anything unique to your association. Next, determine your audience's preference for arrival, departure, and free time.

For example, if your attendees won't spend money on overnight accommodations, don't start your first session at 8 a.m., on the first day. If you're in a city that has popular attractions, include free time (or you run the risk of attendees ditching your sessions). Schedule adjournment immediately following a popular event to ensure most of the attendees will stay until the end.

Educational sessions are scheduled either consecutively (one at a time) or concurrently (more than one session at a time) and should be arranged so that every attendee will get the maximum benefit from the choices. When you have concurrent sessions, scrutinize the topics from the perspective of each attendee and ask yourself whether you are offering something for everyone in each time slot. Be sure topics do not conflict.

For example, the XYZ Association represents companies that send the president, sales managers, and support staff to the convention. The following breakout sessions would provide a choice for each type of attendee, as well as one they can attend together.

TOPIC	TARGET AUDIENCE
The Keys to Closing a Sale	Sales managers
Teamwork for Today	All attendees
Putting Your Overweight Budget on a Diet	President
Maximizing Your Use of Technology	Support staff

What you want to accomplish will dictate the length of your sessions. In-depth topics with lots of hands-on participation will require more time. An update requires less. Adult learning trends point toward sessions that focus on learning rather than teaching. (No more speakers standing up front and talking for 90 minutes!) Sessions ranging from 60 to 90 minutes provide time for both speaker and audience participation. Two hours can also be scheduled, but make sure the speaker has plans to keep the audience involved.

Movement time between sessions is often overlooked. Schedule a minimum of 10 minutes for people to move from one session or event to the next. More time is preferable, however, so attendees have time to go to the bathroom, take a smoking break, get something to drink or eat, or simply talk with one another and the speakers. Include longer time blocks for networking, visiting the trade show, and free time.

Meals can include simply eating, eating and listening, or eating and doing. If you're planning a meal just for eating, schedule an hour or less; 45 minutes is fine if you ask the hotel to preset the salad and dessert (have it on the table when guests arrive to eat). Meals for eating and listening may include a keynote speaker, awards presentations, or entertainment. Plan a bathroom break between the meal and the presentation.

Meals that include an activity—such as visiting the trade show or participating in a fundraiser—are often served as a boxed meal or a reception with heavy hors d'oeuvres (lots of appetizers that serve as the meal). Allow time for people to move through the food lines, get a drink, mingle, and participate in any activities you offer. If you're scheduling the meal in the trade show, include the exhibitors in all activities and food functions.

Conventions often revolve around themes. Some themes thread throughout the event; others are simply used for meals or special events. Themes can be fun and will draw people together if you plan activities, the trade show, and the meals to revolve around them. One word of caution, however: Using a theme can cost more in props, decorations, and labor for set-up, so budget accordingly.

A sample agenda for the XYZ Association's 79th Annual Convention and Trade Show might look like this:

Monday, November 7

8:00-10:15 a.m.	Board of Directors meeting
10:30 a.m.-Noon	Opening General Session and Year-In-Review
Noon-1:30 p.m.	Trade Show opens (with boxed lunch in hall)
1:30-3:00 p.m.	Breakout sessions (four topics offered)
3:00-3:30 p.m.	Refreshment break in the Trade Show
3:30-5:00 p.m.	Breakout sessions (four topics offered)
6:30-8:00 p.m.	President's Theme Reception in the Trade Show, "A Technological Dream"

Tuesday, November 8

8:00-8:30 a.m	Continental Breakfast in Trade Show
8:30-10:00 a.m.	Breakout sessions (four topics offered)
10:00 a.m.-12:30 p.m.	Tours of nearby local attractions or free time
10:15-11:45 a.m.	Personal enhancement or entertaining sessions for those not on tours (for example—learn about wine tasting or money management)
12:30-1:30 p.m.	Lunch and Annual Business meeting
1:30-2:30 p.m.	Trade Show open (with dessert in hall)
2:30-4:00 p.m.	Breakout sessions (four topics offered)
5:30-6:30 p.m.	Reception
6:30-9:30 p.m.	Dinner, Awards Banquet, and Entertainment

Wednesday, November 9

No events planned

Publicity and Registration

All your efforts will be wasted if no one comes to your meeting. Publicity must happen early. It doesn't have to be expensive, just timely and thorough. Your goal is to convince potential attendees to register, so be sure to include several benefit statements. (For example: As an attendee you will learn five new ways to increase sales.)

Following is a basic publicity timetable.

PUBLICITY ITEM	DATE DISTRIBUTED	DETAILS TO INCLUDE
Announce date and location	At the previous year's event or as soon as it's confirmed.	The date and the location so people can put it on their calendars. Run the announcement in your current convention's program book, in your magazine or newsletter, in e-mails—in everything that leaves the association office.
Date saver	6–9 months prior	Date, location, and event highlights if you have finalized something that is a real draw, such as a well-known speaker or a special event.
Prospectus (registration packet)	About 6 weeks before the early registration deadline.	The registration form with benefit statements and • an agenda-at-a-glance so readers can easily see the convention layout (put this first) • a list of all sessions (with speaker names and descriptions if possible), special events, and other activities • a list of exhibitors and sponsors that are booked to date • hotel reservation information and directions • event and speaker highlights, if space permits • anything else you think will convince them to register
Reminder card or letter	Two weeks before the early registration deadline	The date and location may be a highlight, but emphasize the increased registration rate that happens after the early deadline.
Advertising	Ongoing	Publicize your convention in every issue of your magazine, in industry calendars, and at other conventions that tie in to your industry.

Designing a standard registration form will save you time later. In addition to requesting details such as attendee name, title, organization, and address, the form should include:

- An ADA statement ("If you have special dietary requirements or a disability that requires special accommodations or assistance to attend this events, please list them here: _____.") Be sure to follow-up on these requests and provide the meals or special services for those who request them.
- The CEU (Continuing Education Unit) information or CME (Continuing Medical Education) credit awarded to the participant,

if your industry requires verification of continuing education. Note whether your association is an approved provider through a credentialing agency or association. List the provider number if it is a requirement of your agreement as a provider.

- A statement of no guarantee for on-site registration space, hand-outs, or name badges (for a CE event).

- Your cancellation policy. Outline what portion, if any, of the registration fee will be refunded if a registrant cancels. Also note when the registrant should expect the refund—before or after the event.

- Registration deadlines for early bird registration (at discounted fees), conference registrations, and hotel reservations.

If everything goes as planned, once you mail your prospectus you will have registration forms coming back that need attention. Even if you are a one-person office, set up a system for processing the registrations that includes checks and balances.

Only process registrations that are complete and accurate—the ones that include complete information and are paid correctly. Put the incorrect registrations in a problem folder and work with the registrant to correct it in advance. It is far easier to solve problems before your convention than on site. Aim to have all registrations accurately processed at least one week before the event.

Working with Speakers

One of your first tasks is to identify and hire speakers. Managing speaker details can take some time, especially if you hire many. To ensure each speaker understands what you want and you understand what the speaker needs from you, confirm everything in writing, use a speaker agreement, and send a confirmation right before your event.

If you hire professional speakers, consider using a *speaker's bureau.* The speaker's bureau representative will interview you to determine your meeting needs and event objectives. He or she will then provide you with a list of speakers whose fees are within your budget, as well as videotapes and support material for you to review. You do not pay for these services.

If you are hiring industry professionals, call them directly. When you invite a potential speaker, describe your event and its objective; the topic you want him or her to cover; the day, date, time, and location of the presentation; and the compensation. Although many industry professionals do not charge to speak, compensation may include an *honorarium* (fee for speaking); complimentary conference registration, meals, or a per-diem (a set amount given to cover expenses); and mileage reimbursement (check the IRS web site at www.irs.gov for the current rate).

Following verbal confirmation, send a letter and speaker agreement that lists the agreed-upon details and asks about the speaker needs. Ask the speaker to return the form at least four weeks before the event. After you've received the completed speaker agreement, send a confirmation that includes a description of how the room will be set (including a list of audiovisual equipment), the name of the room monitor, and a copy of the speaker's introduction. Give the speaker the opportunity to make corrections before your event.

Booking hotel and airline reservations for your speakers is a gracious gesture but will take a lot of time. You might ask the speakers to handle their own arrangements and then bill you. You can even offer to reimburse any expenses that are charged to a credit card when the charge is made rather than waiting until after the event.

If you choose to handle the speaker's hotel accommodations, ask for arrival and departure dates and create a *rooming list* for the hotel. This is a list of guests whose rooms will be billed to the master account. Include their names, arrival and departure dates, and the expenses the association will cover (all charges or just room, tax, and parking). Agreeing to cover all charges opens you to the possibility that someone will watch movies, order room service, or make long-distance calls at your expense. If you agree to pay room, tax, and parking, ask the speaker to bill you separately for his or her additional reimbursable expenses such as meals.

If you prefer that the association handles speakers' airline reservations, direct your speakers to a trusted travel agent who will make their reservations and then bill the association.

Having numerous speakers may indicate the need for a *speaker ready room*. This provides a central location for you to meet and communicate with all of your speakers and for them to use to store materials, have refreshments, practice their presentations, or simply relax. If you have an extra room to devote to that purpose, it's a nice gesture, as well as a convenience for you, the speakers, and the room monitors. If your budget allows, include a laptop computer so speakers can review their presentations in the ready room.

Function Sheets

Two people need to know every detail of your convention—you and your hotel contact. You communicate these details on a function sheet, which is also known as a Banquet Event Order (BEO). You can talk through all your details, write them in memo format, or use a form. The form is the safest and easiest because both parties have a written document, which results in fewer mistakes.

Be accurate with all of your details, numbers, and times. The information you give to your convention services manager or catering manager (the hotel representative who will coordinate your event) will be recorded on the hotel's BEOs, sent to you for review, and then distributed to every hotel department. Every staff member involved will have the information. Changes can certainly be made, but having the BEO as close to accurate the first time is helpful.

The function sheet will include space for you to describe how to set up each meeting and event room. The hotel knows the best way to set its rooms in standard set-ups. You just need to indicate the style you would like for each event. Following are standard room sets and their possible uses.

STYLE	DESCRIPTION	USES
Theater	Chairs in rows facing the speaker	Short breakout sessions
Classroom	Chairs with tables facing the speaker	Longer breakout sessions or all-day events
Conference block	Large table(s) with chairs on the perimeter	Small board or committee meetings
Hollow square	Tables set in a square or rectangle with chairs on the perimeter	Large board or committee meetings
U-shape	Tables set in a U (one side open) with chairs on the perimeter. Chairs can be set on the inside of the U for larger groups.	Sessions or meetings that feature a speaker or audiovisual presentations
Rounds	Round tables with chairs	Meal functions; sessions that require small group interaction
Flow	No furniture, just space. Small cocktail tables may be scattered around the room.	Receptions

Your function sheet should also include other equipment you might need in the room, such as a lectern (table-top or free-standing), registration desk, and table numbers (used when you have assigned seating). Also include the equipment that takes up extra space such as a riser, dance floor, extra tables for materials, or excessive audiovisual equipment. These all affect the total number of tables or seats that will fit in the room.

Food

Menu selection for a group can be tricky. No matter how hard you try, you will not please everyone. Consider having the chef or catering manager select your menus—this person knows the facility's specialties, what's in season, and what groups generally enjoy. Present a list of your meal events and your per-person cost and ask the hotel to provide suggestions. In addition to the food costs, the hotel will add close to 20 percent gratuity, as well as tax. A $14.95 lunch could cost $19.02 ($14.95 + 18% gratuity + 7.75% tax). Because of this, list your per-person cost and indicate that it is *inclusive* (including gratuity and tax).

If you make your own menu selections, choose a combination of foods—in other words, don't serve beef at every meal. If you choose unusual items, offer alternatives; for example, instead of serving only red snapper, serve a duet of red snapper and a petit filet. To stay within your budget, figure the total (inclusive) costs for each selection.

A popular misconception is that buffets are cheaper than plated meals. In fact, buffets may be more expensive because the hotel puts out more food. If your hotel quotes a lower rate for a buffet, ask how many servers will be scheduled. A plated meal will have about one server for every 20 guests. A buffet should have similar staffing because the only work buffet servers don't do is set the plates in front of guests. Fewer servers could result in slow beverage and clearing service.

Hotels will require guarantees about three business days before each catered event. At that time, you submit the number of people you plan to serve. You can increase the number but not decrease it. Catering departments plan for a small percentage over (about 5 percent) for last-minute additions. Some meeting planners use this flexibility to save food and money by under guaranteeing (guaranteeing for fewer people than are expected).

Say, for example, you have sold 132 tickets to your Tuesday night dinner and awards banquet. If you guarantee 132, you have to pay for 132 even if 129 meals are served. You could also reduce that number slightly by first assuming there will be at least a few (let's say four) no shows. You're at 128. Then you can reduce that by the hotel's planned overage of 5 percent to reduce your number by 6. Your final guarantee for your 132 tickets would be 122, and the hotel will prepare 128 meals.

Under guaranteeing can be risky. If you have five last-minute guests, there will be no extra meals for them. The hotel will certainly feed them something, but it might not be what you have selected and it could be served much later. A safe way to guarantee is to use the exact number of tickets you have sold or given away. The hotel overage can be used for last-minute ticket sales and other unexpected scenarios.

In addition to the total number of guests, your guarantee should include the types and quantities of special meals you will need—vegetarian, low-salt, kosher, and so forth. You will pull this information from registration forms in the section asking for special needs. Provide these attendees with a card listing their meal requests; they place the cards at their places so servers can easily identify who gets each special meal.

Many guests do not indicate that they need vegetarian meals but assume these will be available. Yet hotels must plan for these just as they do any other entrée. If you think your group will include numerous last-minute requests for vegetarian plates, ask the hotel to prepare additional meals. Ask servers to give the vegetarian meals only to those who have requested them in advance and are identified by the cards. Last-minute requests will then be filled if meals are available.

Audiovisual (A/V) Equipment and Aids

Either the hotel or a separate company will provide the microphones, LCD projectors, overhead projectors, flip charts, and so forth used in sound and visual presentations. Rental usually includes technician support, but you should confirm this in advance.

This support means that a technician is in the hotel and available when you call. He or she will also be on call for any other meetings in the hotel. If you have complex audiovisual requirements, consider hiring a technician exclusively for your event; it's worth the expense when you're faced with concurrent sessions that have concurrent problems.

When you write your function sheets, include a list of the equipment needed for each presentation or event. Audiovisual rental can be expensive. LCD (liquid crystal display) projectors, for example, can cost between $100 and $650 a day and may not include the screen rental. LCDs are typically used to project Microsoft PowerPoint presentations from PC and Mac computers (which you also need to rent if a speaker cannot provide one). LCDs also work with VHS tapes and DVDs when connected to the appropriate player. If you have concurrent sessions, you might rent one LCD for each room. Negotiate a reduced rate if you're using the equipment for more than one day.

Professional speakers will be well-versed in the program and equipment. When using industry speakers, however, ask them to arrive well in advance to test the equipment and practice using it. This is where your audiovisual technician comes in handy.

There is a formula to determine the size of screen you need based on the audience and room size. Leave those calculations to the professionals. Simply list a screen as one of the items you need in a room, and the hotel will provide the appropriate one. As for microphones, the following chart can help you decide which type to request.

TYPE	DESCRIPTION	USE
Lectern	Wired and placed in a holder on a lectern	For speeches from the lectern. The speaker does not move. Good for an emcee or for introductions.
Standing (floor)	Wired and placed in a holder	For use in one place such as an aisle for people to approach and use.
Table	Wired and placed in a holder	For use on a table for speakers, such as panelists who are seated.
Hand-held wireless	Not wired. Can be placed in a holder at the lectern or in an aisle.	For someone who is walking around but doesn't need to use his or her hands. For audience use in a large room.
Lavaliere (lapel)	Wired and clipped to the speaker's clothing.	For someone who is walking around in the front of the room and needs to use his or her hands.
Wireless lavaliere (lapel)	Not wired and clipped to the speaker's clothes	For someone who is walking around the room a lot. (Note: Ask for fresh batteries in the equipment and an extra set for back-up.)

Signage and Transportation

Think of signs as tools for your attendees. You may know your way around a venue, but they don't. Attendees appreciate having signs to point them in the right direction.

You may need just one sign for one-day events. This can be a small sign placed on an easel near your registration desk. If you have a nice one made with your association logo, you can use it for all of your events. You may want a second sign for the hotel entrance if the property is big. Multi-day events require additional signage that may include the following:

- Welcome (one for the hotel entrance and one for the registration desk).

- Registration desk signs to point attendees to the correct line if necessary.

- Sponsor signs that list the names (and logos, if possible) of all contributing companies.

- Directional signs to place throughout the property identifying rooms and how to get there.

- Room signs listing times and names of events that will be in the room.

Even a small meeting might need 10 or more signs and, unless your signs are generic, you'll use them once and discard them. One low-cost choice is to design your signs on your computer and have a local sign company enlarge and mount them on foam core. The sign company can also create a nice banner that the hotel will hang for you in the lobby or a general session room (put it on your function sheet). If you make the banner generic with your association name and logo, you can use it for numerous events.

If your attendees fly to the meeting, work with an airline to offer them reduced rates. Contact the airline with a hub at your destination and ask for the group travel coordinator. You may also need to arrange for ground transportation—the buses and other vehicles used for shuttling attendees from one point to another for off-site events. Depend on the expertise of the bus company representatives to figure out schedules and bus sizes.

Getting Help

Although you will do most of your convention planning on your own, other people and services can support you throughout the process.

PERSON OR SERVICE	WHAT THEY ARE	WHAT THEY CAN HELP WITH
Convention and Visitors Bureau	A local nonprofit agency that promotes tourism to the area	• distribute your RFP and identify appropriate venues • provide a list of local speakers, entertainers, and suppliers • provide hostess service • provide complimentary printed materials and maps of the area
Sales Manager	The hotel representative who booked your meeting	• discuss best use of space for each of your events
Catering Manager	The hotel representative who coordinated all aspects of your meeting	• budgeting for food, audiovisual rental, staffing • menu selection • guarantees • special event planning, set up, and execution
Show decorator	The company that does your trade show set up	• budgeting for exhibits • space use • set-up and tear-down times • special event ideas and execution • drayage (storing and delivering boxes)
Committee members	Volunteers who should be committed to making the event a success	• agenda development • fee structure • topic and speaker selection • on-site assistance (especially as room monitors)
Industry suppliers	Companies that provide materials to meeting managers	• name badge stock and holders • tent cards and other materials • advertising novelties and other gift items
Other meeting professionals	Meeting planners who have done it before—your predecessor, colleagues in other states or in other local associations, and independent planners	• consulting on all aspects of your event • contract language • planning tips • hotel bookings

Continues on next page

PERSON OR SERVICE	WHAT THEY ARE	WHAT THEY CAN HELP WITH
Meeting industry Web sites	Web sites that support the association and/or meetings industry	• lots of tips and forms
Google or other Internet search engines	Internet tool that searches for information you identify (example: go to www.google.com, key in "number of cups of coffee in a gallon," and it leads you to Planning Beverage Breaks, a page on the site for the Professional Convention Management Association. Answer: 20 cups)	• everything else you need—key in any question and you will be led to sites that have answers

You might also consider:

- Working with a professional entertainment broker to identify and hire entertainers for your event.

- Hiring a company to decorate rooms for special events. Using centerpieces, props, and other materials, the decorator can create any theme or atmosphere you request. It comes with a price tag, of course, but it takes a lot off your hands.

- Ordering centerpieces from a florist; you can then give away the centerpieces at the end of the event. Florists can also provide potted plants and trees that make a stage look more professional and eye catching.

- Using the hotel's decorations, provided as part of its meetings services. A hotel can decorate break tables to match a theme using supplies they own—such as beach balls, sand pails, and sunglasses for a beach theme. Hotels can also provide basic centerpieces (typically mirrors, candles, or artificial flower arrangements).

Sponsors

Event sponsors are a source of income to the association. Your event provides a good opportunity to thank sponsors for their support and to showcase their contributions. Before soliciting sponsors, create a sponsor prospectus that lists the various events that can be sponsored. There are three basic sponsorship categories:

Convention underwriters contribute to the overall event budget. You can establish levels of giving or accept any amount a company is willing to offer. Thank these sponsors as a group as often as possible in signs, in the program book, on slides in general sessions, in announcements, and anywhere your attendees will be gathered.

Activity underwriters pick up the cost of a specific event such as a lunch, a coffee break, or a speaker. You determine the cost of each event and what you want to solicit from a sponsor—either all or a portion of the costs. Thank these sponsors individually at the event or session they sponsor, in the program book with the event listing, and on slides at the events. Invite them to greet attendees at the event or introduce the speaker.

Attendee enhancement sponsors purchase gifts or other giveaways that don't underwrite any of your expenses but enhance your attendees' convention experience. Examples include customized canvas bags, bottled water, lined paper, pens, mugs (put out for coffee breaks and then distributed to guests), sticky notes, and industry items (such as product samples). Companies typically imprint their logos on these items and give them to you to distribute to each attendee.

Regardless of their contribution, all sponsors should be thanked appropriately in public and personally. Immediately after the event, say thank you again by listing all event contributors in your magazine or newsletter or on your Web site.

Crisis Management

It is unlikely that you will have to handle a crisis at an association event. Still, things happen: Power is lost, people get sick (or even die), and bad weather develops—all occurrences you should be prepared to handle.

When preparing for a crisis, the first step is to brainstorm possible problems and their solutions. Typical crises that you may face include speaker cancellation, loss of power or technical failure, weather-related delays or consequences, medical emergencies, and food-related illnesses. Others include fire, major acts of God, terrorism, and loss of service staff due to strike. If you have a plan for the more common crisis, you will be prepared to adapt it to any crisis with which you're faced.

Venue staff usually handle on-site emergencies, but confirm this before your meeting. A facility such as a banquet hall or university building with few staff may not have the trained personnel of a hotel.

A medical emergency is probably your most likely crisis—for example, a diabetic can lose consciousness or someone can have a heart attack. To ensure swift response to medical emergencies, print the following on the back of your name badges and ask everyone (staff, speakers, and exhibitors) to fill it in as soon as they pick up their registrant packets:

Emergency contact name
Emergency contact day number
Emergency contact evening number
Medical conditions
Allergies

One crisis that could affect your entire event is if you, the sole planner, becomes incapable of doing your job. This could happen in the middle of planning or in the middle of the event itself. Your back-up for this is to keep thorough notes that are easy to locate in your files or computer (make sure it's not password protected). Assign a back-up person who can step in if needed. Put together an on-site convention manual for you, any assistants, and your back-up person; the manual should contain function sheets, speaker introductions, scheduling notes, and key contact names and phone numbers.

Next, identify a crisis management team that includes the following people:

- A decision maker—one person who decides how to respond.
- A coordinator to act as liaison to all parties—hotel, emergency responders, and staff.
- An attendee liaison to communicate with attendees.
- A spokesperson to speak to the media or public, if necessary.
- A transcriber to record everything that happens.

Your goal during any crisis is to put safety first, remain calm, and take charge of your plan.

On-Site Implementation

By the time you're on site you will have planned everything. The hotel knows what you need and will provide it. The speakers know where they're going and will show up. The audiovisual technicians have your list of equipment and will set it up properly.

Unfortunately, glitches will always occur. You forgot that one speaker changed her mind and wanted a flip chart instead of a whiteboard. An attendee insists that he requested a vegetarian meal. A speaker arrives with his original handout and expects you to copy it—now.

As a small office you don't have co-workers to fall back on so you have to be creative with staffing to handle these glitches. It is essential that you assign tasks to everyone but yourself so that you are available to respond to issues as they arise. You are the master choreographer on site; you can't be a principal dancer, too.

In addition to any co-workers you have, you can use the following. Offer them complimentary event registrations in exchange for their work.

- Association members, especially board members and committee members.
- Students who are studying your industry.
- Interns—bring one on board to help plan if possible.
- The convention and visitors bureau's hostess service.
- Family members.

In addition, the hotel staff can help you. You will already know two people at the venue—the sales manager who booked your meeting and assigned space and your convention services (or catering) manager who worked with you on your function sheets. Once you're on site you will have a *pre-con (pre-convention) meeting,* during which key hotel personnel meet you and review the details of your event (such as who is authorized to sign for expenditures to the master account).

Your sales manager will lead the meeting, which includes a review of every function sheet with the catering manager, the audiovisual technician, and the banquet captain (the person who manages events on the floor). At this point, you ensure that the staff has interpreted your requirements correctly and that you understand how the hotel will execute your requests. Ask a lot of questions and make changes as needed. It's always easier to do this in advance than at the last minute.

Even though you have accurately outlined your requirements, check the room set-ups on the day of your event. Even for one-day events this may mean walking through the rooms at 5:30 a.m., when you might catch an error before speakers or attendees arrive. Refer to your function sheets to check that everything you requested is in place. Meals and special events that happen later in the day will be set well in advance so plan to look at the room as set-up proceeds and make changes if necessary.

It can be helpful to everyone—you, the speakers, and the attendees—to assign a monitor to each session. The monitor will check the room set-up, assist the speaker as needed, distribute handouts (and continuing education forms, if needed), introduce the speaker, and collect evaluation forms.

You can assign monitors to each session or to each room. Assigning by room requires much less recruiting, but requires the monitor to stay in the room all day, regardless of the topic. A short training for all room monitors is helpful. In large sessions, room monitors should be instructed to get help distributing and collecting material and assisting if needed.

Registration Desk

The registration desk is the first place attendees will visit when they arrive at your event and where they will get their first impressions. Staffing must be adequate and welcoming: No grumpy people at the registration desk!

Have a plan in place to ensure a smooth registration process, especially during the rush times. Know how you will process pre-registered attendees, on-site registrations, ticket sales, name badge corrections, and miscellaneous problems. Ensure that money is carefully recorded at every step. It is a good practice to have one person assigned to the money so too many hands don't muddle the process.

Use a numbered receipt book to record all money accepted and a cash-out receipt to record all money removed. A cash-out receipt is as simple as the following that you have copied at your office and stuck in the cash box.

XYZ Association
CASH-OUT RECEIPT

Date: _____

Amount Taken: $ _____

Taken by _____

For _____

NOTES: _____

_____

Stocking the registration desk of a one-day meeting requires fewer supplies, but no less attention, than a multi-day event. Store these supplies in a box that you can take with you each time you go to an event (a fishing tackle box is handy for this). Restock the box after each event, and grab it as you walk out the door for your next meeting.

- Event registration forms and brochures.
- Attendee roster (3 copies).
- Receipt book with numbered receipts.
- Pens (bring a lot; they are always taken).
- Attendee name badges, printed in alphabetical order, and holders.
- Blank name badges and extra holders.
- Markers.
- Sticky notes.
- Pad of lined paper.
- Paper clips.
- Knife or blade to open boxes.
- Calculator.
- Index cards.
- Miscellaneous comfort items (aspirin, tissue, cough drops, and so forth).

For a multi-day meeting, add the following:

- More pens.
- More pads of lined paper.
- Cash box with cash for change.
- A ream of white paper.
- Stapler with extra staples.
- Tape.
- Rubber bands.
- Highlighters.
- Computer loaded with a copy of the registration records and planning files.
- Printer (to make your life easier).

The Aftermath

You may experience a sense of let-down after a major event. A one-day event is merely another version of your work day, but a multi-day event which you have been working on for months is like your child. In fact, the execution of a convention has been compared to birthing a baby: Lots of planning and expectations and then, suddenly, it's all over.

Don't be lulled into thinking you can finally relax (or collapse from exhaustion) after the completion of your event. You still need to take care of the follow-up details—which are just as important as the pre-convention details.

Giving Thanks. Many people helped make your event a success. Send letters of thanks to hotel staff (including the general manager, your sales manager, and your catering manager), sponsors, speakers, and exhibitors. Be specific in your praise and constructive with any criticism. Hotels and speakers use your comments as references for future bookings and appreciate genuine praise, as well as criticism that is deserved and presented fairly.

If you can afford it, distributing gratuities to hotel staff is a traditional way to express your appreciation for a job well done. There are different thoughts on when to give a gratuity—before the event so people will work hard for you or after the event to thank those who put forth lots of effort. The former might be construed as a bribe. The latter plan is especially effective at venues that you frequent. Hotel staffs remember kind meeting professionals and are pleased to return the favor.

If you can, give cash gratuities; put them in envelopes with personal messages written on association stationery. Hand them out personally and with a kind word. Deciding who should receive a gratuity can be tough. Here is a list of people you should consider:

- Sales manager (give a gift instead of cash).
- Catering manager (be generous).
- Banquet captains (be generous).
- Housemen (if you required many different room set-ups or changes).
- Bellmen (if you required a lot of help or your attendees are not tippers).
- Housekeepers (if you know your attendees required a lot of attention).
- PBX/phone operators (if you used them a lot).

- Front desk staff (if they went out of their way for you or your attendees).
- Concierge (if he or she helped you a lot).

If you don't have the budget for cash gratuities, write personalized notes or letters to each person who helped you or your attendees. In addition, write a letter to the general manager and key department heads praising people by name and explaining why you are pleased with their service.

Assessing. A formal assessment will serve as your guide for planning next year's event. Start the process by distributing evaluation forms to attendees and exhibitors. Create one form to assess the overall event, another to assess each speaker, and a third for the exhibitors to assess the trade show.

Only ask questions for which you truly want a response or to which you can actually respond. For example, don't ask how attendees liked the food (unless it's very important for you or the hotel to know). Don't ask them to rate the hotel if you plan to use a different one. Do ask if their expectations were met and what they would do differently if they could plan the event. Summarizing the comments requires a lot of time so consider outsourcing the task to a student, intern, or committee volunteer.

You will receive many wonderful comments and a few biting ones. You'll hear from the extremes—good and bad. To make the comments productive, look for trends—don't change the timing of your sessions, for example, based on one or two comments. Remember that most people don't say anything at all because they are satisfied.

In addition to participant input, assess the event from the planning perspective. Ask your committee members to evaluate the following:

- Objective—did you fulfill your event objective?
- Execution—what went smoothly and what didn't? What did you like and what didn't you like?
- Timing—do the days of the week and the month of the year work for everyone, including exhibitors or suppliers?
- Venue—did the property satisfactorily meet your needs?
- Agenda—did the flow of the agenda and its individual events work?
- Registration desk—did the process flow smoothly?

- Trade show—did the association, the attendees, and the exhibitors benefit from the show?

- Meals and special events—did they serve their purpose?

- Budget—was it realistic?

Reviewing the Master Account. After the hotel closes your account, you will receive the master bill that lists all charges from sleeping rooms, banquets, and miscellaneous services. The bill is typically supported by *guest folios* (forms that list transactions by room) and *banquet checks* (forms that list charges for each event). Be sure to review every charge, even for one-day events. It is easy to make errors, and you're the only one who will recognize them. Discuss the errors with your catering manager and agree on how they will be corrected. Ask for a new statement and pay from that.

Planning Timelines

Planning timelines can be found on many meeting planning Web sites. Each meeting is different, however, and everyone works at a different pace. It's better to create your own tool to track your tasks and progress. You might find that it's easier to complete something in its entirety than to do its separate tasks based on the calendar. For example, you might prefer to write and design all of your publicity material in December rather than design the date saver in January, the prospectus in May, and the reminder card in October.

No matter what method you use, a summary of tasks is helpful. Here are the basic tasks to include on your list:

1. **Determine your objective**—why have the meeting?
2. **Identify the target audience**—who will attend?
3. **Choose a venue**—what facility will allow you to fulfill your objectives and meet the needs of your audience?
4. **Sketch out the agenda**—what do you want to accomplish during the event? How many days will it take to complete them?
5. **Pick a date**—what days of the week will fit the agenda, the needs of your audience, and your budget? What month will do the same?
6. **Create a budget**—budget conservatively for income and generously for expenses. Create an expense budget that is specific to the venue, your speakers, and so forth.

7. **Fill in the content**—finalize the agenda with session titles, meals and special events. Hire your speakers and entertainers.

8. **Get out the publicity**—let your audience know about the event and offer simple ways for them to register.

9. **Start planning**—initiate the tasks that will ensure a successful event, including communicating with all involved parties.

10. **Manage the event**—make it happen by executing all of your plans.

11. **Conduct follow-up tasks**—evaluate the event and your planning efforts, as well as thank the event contributors.

Remember, to some members, your meetings *are* the association. Good meetings provide many tangible and intangible benefits. Your time is well spent planning meetings that are well thought-out in content and presentation.

Note: These meeting planning forms, available on the accompanying CD-ROM, can be customized to your association's needs:

- Annual Convention Budget Worksheet
- Annual Convention Event History Form
- Annual Convention Sample RFP
- Banquet Event Order
- Conference Evaluation Form
- Conference Speaker Information Confirmation
- Convention Monitor Training Handout
- Event Function Sheet
- Sample Hotel Rooming List
- Session Monitor's Checklist
- Speaker Agreement Form
- Speaker Guidelines
- Speaker Biographical and Seminar Information
- Speaking Meeting Room Requirements
- Speaker Housing and Travel Arrangements
- Speaker Reimbursement Policies
- Speaker Request Form
- Statement for Professional Services

Assessing Technology Needs

By Peter S. Weber, CAE

I T IS HARD TO imagine a modern association office without the productivity, security, ease-of-use, and mobility that are possible with office technology. Developments and advances in technology are constantly creating new opportunities for more efficient business operations. At the same time, these rapid developments make it challenging for executives of small staff associations to determine how to invest their technology budget wisely.

To make technology work for your staff and your members, develop an office technology plan that is regularly assessed and updated. To guide your efforts, refer to the following *Professional Practice Statement on Developing a Technology Plan* issued by Association Forum of Chicagoland (reprinted with permission from Association Forum of Chicagoland):

> *Policy Statement:* Every association should consider having a strategic technology plan. The plan should be a cohesive, integrated one that extends beyond computer systems to include and integrate all communications, information, and operational processing technologies. The association's strategic technology plan should identify standards and systems that will improve and enhance the core business processes. It should parallel the organization's business plan so that it becomes a tool to further the organizational mission, goals, and strategies and avoids becoming an end in itself.
>
> *Professional Practices for Executives:* The plan should be developed under the direction of the association executive and his or her staff and should include:
>
> • A time frame, generally two to three years.

- A vision for technology that matches the organization's business information and operational needs, including systems, components or chapters, staffing, and overall resource allocation.
- An assessment of the organization's business and operational requirements, taking into account existing technology, the strengths and weaknesses of both, and their ability to work in synergy to meet current needs.
- A statement of need that includes broad descriptions of the types of systems needed to further strategic goals.
- A statement of goals to achieve new technological capacity and changes required within the current system to reach capacity.
- A statement of objectives, including return on investment, and how they will be measured or evaluated.
- In-depth research to identify all technologies available or likely to become available during the duration of the plan, including cost analyses.
- Identification of those technologies to be included in the plan.
- Iteration of actions and attendant costs required to implement the plan, including:
  - New technology acquisition
  - Creating and implementing interfaces with existing technology
  - Phase-out of obsolete technologies
  - Organizational standards for technology use by staff and membership
  - Staff training
  - Implementation priorities, time frames, and budgets.
  - Selection of individual(s) to oversee implementation and evaluation
  - Ongoing evaluation mechanisms to ensure that technologies are used to their fullest potential and that the organization receives adequate return on investment
  - A system of reassessment to ensure adequacy and applicability
  - A goal to update the plan to keep pace with changes in critical business strategies

The plan should be an inclusive process that engages the enthusiasm, support, and understanding of the membership, the governing bodies, the staff, and technology partners. It should take advantage of organizational expertise, knowledge, and experience.

Professional Practices for the Governing Body: The governing body should:

- Regard the development of technology plan for the association as essential to its success.
- Ensure integration of the plan into the association's broader strategic plan.
- Support implementation of the plan at every level of the organization.
- Use the plan to focus the technology agenda of the organization.
- Use the plan to inform financial forecasting and integrate it with the annual budgeting process.
- Use the plan to focus resources on key technologies critical to organizational success.
- Update the plan regularly to ensure its relevance to the needs of the organization.

Buying Desktop Computers

Part of developing your technology plan is surveying the available technology and determining what hardware and productivity tools will help you achieve your technology goals.

Most office technology purchases begin with the desktop computer. For the vast majority of business applications, the newest and latest high-speed microprocessors, which boast speeds in excess of 4GHz, are more than you need. In fact, many business users save money by investing in machines with slightly slower Celeron or AMD chips.

If speed is really important to you, invest in extra random access memory (RAM). RAM is the most common type of computer memory, in which the computer stores system software, programs, and data currently being used. Consider upgrading to a minimum of 512MB of RAM. If you run multiple software applications at once, that additional memory will keep your programs running quickly and efficiently.

On the other hand, you probably don't need a huge hard drive. Home PC users may clutter their hard drives with MP3 downloads, digital photos, and home videos. At work, however, a standard hard drive offers plenty of space for most users. If your office technology plan includes the purchase of a network server, the need for large desktop hard drives is even further mitigated.

If, however, your association works with video or large graphics files, you'll need more memory in your system. In addition to lots of RAM, you'll want a larger hard drive, FireWire and USB 2.0 connectors, and a separate graphics card with its own memory as opposed to one integrated on the motherboard.

Do You Need to Network?

If your association has more than one computer, chances are that you would benefit from networking them. A local area network (LAN) is a computer network limited to the immediate area—often the same building or floor of a building. A LAN connects your association's computers, allowing them to share and exchange a variety of information. While one computer can be useful on its own, two or more computers in a shared environment are much more productive.

A network can benefit your association through:

File Sharing. A network makes it easy for everyone to access the same file and prevents people from accidentally creating different versions. Besides, you won't have to worry about organizing drawers full of floppy disks and CDs.

Printer Sharing. With a network, several computers can share the same printer. Although you might need a more expensive printer to handle the additional workload, it's usually cheaper to use a network printer than to buy separate printers for each desktop workstation.

Collaboration and Communication. It's hard for people to work together if no one knows what anyone else is doing. A network allows employees to share files, view other employees' work, and exchange information efficiently. In a slightly larger office, or if you maintain a remote connection to your office network—for example, you connect your home computer to the office network through a virtual private network—you might use e-mail and instant messaging to communicate quickly and store information for future access.

Greater Organization. A variety of network scheduling software is available to arrange meetings using a shared calendar. This type of software usually includes other tools that will share address books and create to-do lists.

Easier Online Access. If you have several computers but only one or two phone lines, a network makes using the Internet much easier. Several computers can share one Internet connection through the use of a modem and router. You can even install a dedicated high-speed Internet connection (such as cable modem or DSL) for your network.

Data Back-up. No technology plan is complete without a schedule for backing up your data. A network makes it easier to save a copy of your association's data on one set of tapes, CDs, or other backup system.

Just a few years ago, there was only one option for networking your office computers. You paid someone to run Ethernet cables throughout your office, and the cables all plugged into your network hub. Wireless networking technology has become more common in recent years. Both networking options can be used with relatively inexpensive hardware requirements.

Ethernet remains the most widely used networking option. If you are connecting a few stationary systems in the same room or have easy access to overhead or sub-floor conduits, it is probably still the way to go. Ethernet offers the fastest speeds, the lowest cost, and the highest reliability. Almost every new PC has a built-in Ethernet port, and you can find PCI cards or USB adapters for just a few dollars to add Ethernet capability to older computers. Ethernet hubs and switches are equally affordable and can be connected together (daisy-chained) when you run out of ports.

Just make sure all your hubs, switches, and network cards support Fast Ethernet (or 100Mbps)—older equipment may support only the 10Mbps standard. If you want to move huge files quickly, then consider spending a bit more for Gigabit Ethernet (1,000Mbps).

Wireless networking, however, is becoming a simpler and cheaper option for many businesses—especially if you need to create a network that spans a large area or is located in an older building where running Ethernet cables through the walls is costly and arduous. The only choice for your wireless local area network (LAN) is Wi-Fi; 802.11g is recommended for small associations because it combines the best of both worlds: the speed of 802.11a and the range of (and compatibility with) the more prevalent 802.11b.

It is possible to build an inexpensive, basic network with an access point or a hub and a few adapters. This approach, however, has limitations and poses a security risk because it exposes all of your PCs directly to the Internet.

Instead, small associations should start with a router/gateway that includes an 802.11g access point and a firewall. Usually up to four PCs or Macs located close to the router/gateway can be connected directly to the built-in switch or hub using Ethernet cables; you can add systems to the wireless network via a wireless adapter. These come in PCI, USB, PC Card, and even CompactFlash and SD formats, and are relatively inexpensive. Be sure to buy networking gear that supports the latest security standards, such as WPA (Wireless Protected Access).

To meet growing expectations on a limited budget, you'll need to do more with less. That may mean accommodating staff who want—or need—to work from a remote location. A virtual private network (VPN) may be the way to go to maintain fast, secure, and reliable communication with your office computer network regardless of location.

A VPN is a private network that uses a public network (usually the Internet) to connect remote sites or users. VPNs allow staff to have access to the same information that they would have on their office computers—such as the capability to send and receive e-mail messages, organize folders, use the calendar, maintain a contacts list, and so forth. Say it's the weekend and you need to develop a list of sponsors: A VPN allows you to have access to your database without setting foot in the office. You can access your office desktop computer as well as your association's shared drive.

Setting up a VPN is simple and inexpensive. First, you'll need to set up a domain name for your VPN. You can choose to use a free service (such as Dynamic Network Services, Inc., Worcester, MA) or a paid service. As for equipment, you'll need to purchase VPN routers for each location using the VPN (including your association office). The VPN routers are only slightly more expensive than standard routers.

If you're intimidated by setting up the VPN yourself, a computer consultant can probably do the job in under an hour. Once established, a VPN is relatively maintenance free. Best of all, it gives your association another dimension of flexibility and efficiency.

Buying a Network Server

Any machine can work as a server, but network server performance counts far more than it does for any desktop or notebook PC. After all, if your server is under too much strain, your whole network will slow down.

Once you notice your network is slow or erratic, don't immediately rip out your PCs, buy an expensive T1, or upgrade to Gigabit Ethernet. First take a close look at your server: Server disk drive and RAM bottlenecks are two of the most common culprits when it comes to network performance problems. Focus your budget on beefing up RAM and disk space before you splurge on items such as fast CPUs or remote management cards.

For your PC, regular IDE (Integrated Drive Electronics) hard drives are fine. But for servers expected to dish up files to multiple users simultaneously or transmit Web pages to the Internet, SCSI (Small Computer System Interface) is almost essential in a server.

Add as many drives as you can to your system. Most entry-level servers support three to six drives, but you can always add more external storage later. You'll need a minimum of three drives to take advantage of RAID (Redundant Array of Inexpensive Disks), which provides 100 percent data integrity in the event that one of those drives crashes. Note that RAID won't help if you have multiple drive crashes, so be sure to invest in—and use—a tape backup system.

When it comes to RAM, the rule (as with PCs) is "more is better." A minimum of 1GB RAM is good for your workgroup server.

Once you've made these decisions, configuring the rest of the system is a snap. For a network CPU, buy the lowest-speed Pentium III or Pentium 4 available. Skip the CD-RW and DVD drives and stick with a CD-ROM; you can always read and write data over the network if necessary. Also, you probably don't need multiple NICs (Network Interface Cards) or a modem.

But don't forget that tape backup unit! If your network crashes, your office burns in a fire, or a tornado hits your town, your investment will be more than justified.

When shopping for a network, expect to spend two to three times the cost of your desktop systems. Because servers are more complex pieces of hardware than regular PCs, service calls are common when, for example, you're trying to add new hard drives to the system. In other words, make sure you receive an adequate support plan. A one-year warranty is standard these days. If you're not comfortable dealing with computer downtime, a few hundred dollars for a three-year warranty is a worthwhile investment. If you have a previous relationship with a major computer vendor, speak to them about your network server needs.

Internet Access & Web Hosting

An inexpensive dial-up account probably won't meet the needs of your growing association, no matter how small it is, especially if you plan to share Internet access. Broadband cable or DSL access is now available in most areas of the United States, and satellite service is usually an option in rural areas.

Once you have a high-speed provider, develop an association Web site and choose a hosting solution. Few small associations have the in-house capability of developing their own full-functioned Web site and hosting their own Web servers internally. Most small associations are better off leaving it to the experts. Research and find a Web developer/host that best meets the needs and budget of your association. If you would like to have some recommendations for these services, you could join the ASAE technology or executive management listservers and ask your small association colleagues about their experiences. You might also call similar associations in your community or in your trade or profession.

The types of Web hosting available to small associations include a broad range of features and support options and a wide range of prices, from free to very expensive, depending on the needs of your business.

Shared hosting means you share a portion of an existing file server with other organizations. *Dedicated hosting* is exactly what it sounds like: You get your own server and 100 percent of its processing power and storage space. With *co-location hosting* you provide everything—hardware and software—and drop off the package at the host's doorstep. The host's job is simply to make sure that the server stays connected to the Internet.

Most small associations choose a shared hosting solution. Typically, the hosts offer several packages based on the number of e-mail accounts, the bandwidth required, and the amount of storage space on the server. These services can range in price from as little as $5 to more than $100 per month. Generally speaking, you get what you pay for in terms of customer support and guaranteed uptime.

Some small associations develop sophisticated Web sites that feature e-commerce (including credit card processing), Web-based applications, and dynamic database driven pages (.asp). Not surprisingly, Web hosts that will accommodate this level of sophistication are also more expensive.

Your technology plan should include some basic guidelines on what you want out of your association Web site. After doing some research, you may be surprised how easy and affordable it is to give your organization an effective Internet presence.

Buying Monitors and Printers

Flat panel monitors are offered as an upgrade in many desktop system packages. The question for associations is whether the additional cost of a flat panel monitor is justified.

LCD (Liquid Crystal Display) monitors offer many advantages over traditional CRT (Cathode Ray Tube) monitors. They are much smaller, making them an excellent choice for small desks and offices. They can display crisp, legible text and images at higher resolutions, meaning that you can fit more information in the same-size display: a 17-inch LCD has about the same viewable area as a 19-inch CRT display. They require less electricity and emit little heat. Finally, they are easier on the eyes because LCD monitors don't need to refresh or redraw the images many times each second the way CRTs do, creating a barely perceptible screen flicker.

CRT monitors are much less expensive, but as long as you can squeeze it into your budget, a flat panel is a worthwhile investment for most small associations. Look for an LCD that has both analog and DVI (Digital Video Input), a wide viewing angle, and a high contrast ratio. Some pricier models include wide-aspect screens, picture-in-picture capability, built-in speakers, and composite and S-Video inputs; most small associations have little need for these extras.

Printer technology hasn't changed much since shortly after office computing began. You still have two basic choices for printers: laser and inkjet.

Laser printers deliver crisp text and graphics at top speeds, and they are less expensive to operate than inkjets. Inkjets offer low-cost color printing, but the cost of ink cartridges and paper can quickly add up. Inkjet printers are also slower than laser printers.

If you plan to network a low-cost black-and-white personal laser printer, first make sure it is network-able. It is best to connect the networked printer to a machine that's always on (your server, for example) via a USB or parallel port and share it through the Windows printer-sharing system. Many models also offer an optional Ethernet card for direct network printing.

For heavier-duty printing needs, consider a true workgroup printer. Not only do these printers operate at nearly double the speed of a high-end personal printer, they typically include built-in Ethernet support for direct network connections and multiple paper trays. If your office is constantly bogged down with people waiting for print jobs to finish, moving up to a workgroup printer—which costs about three times as much as a personal laser printer—is the way to go.

Make Sure You Are Secure

If you've ever experienced a computer virus, you know the expense and headache involved in eradicating it. If you're really unfortunate, you might have lost all of your data or security to a particularly aggressive virus. But as is the case with many computer security problems, these outbreaks could easily have been prevented with careful planning and investment in the right hardware and software.

The first step in securing your office technology doesn't require you to purchase anything. You simply need to make sure that every computer on your network has the latest patches and updates. Both Microsoft Windows XP and Apple Mac OS X include utilities that automatically scan your system, download any updates, and install them.

Next, install a reliable antivirus program and keep it current. McAfee VirusScan and Symantec's Norton AntiVirus are the two most popular products. Antivirus programs rely on a database of virus definition files to recognize and eradicate viruses. When a new one pops up, nearly all of the antivirus companies automatically update their definition files, which is why it is critical to keep your antivirus program updated.

If your network has 10 or more PCs, consider investing in a network solution with multiple client licenses; these protect servers as well as client PCs and include administrative tools so that you can ensure all systems keep an antivirus program installed and up-to-date. All it takes is one weak link to break the entire chain.

Third, build a firewall around your computer network. While antivirus programs are critical, they can't handle all types of security threats. There are two basic types of firewalls—hardware and software—and to be most secure, you should use both. Thanks to the rapid spread of wireless networking, many router/gateways now include hardware firewalls that monitor incoming Internet traffic. For complete protection, add a software-based firewall suitable for small networks. These software applications require nominal configuration to distinguish between legitimate incoming and outgoing traffic and digital trespassers. You'll also find numerous scanning utilities, which probe your network for holes and vulnerabilities, available for free.

Finally, consider investing a few hundred dollars in an independent security consultant who can install these applications and show you how to use them. Security of your data and technology investment should be a top priority in your technology plan.

Adding Software

Most new computers come bundled with a good assortment of software. But there are invaluable software programs that many associations have used for years to operate more efficiently. They include:

- Word processing (to enter and design text).
- Database management (to organize and keep track of large amounts of information).
- Spreadsheets (to organize numerical information and perform calculations).
- Graphics software (to draw, paint, and design pictures and store them on graphic files; and to use graphic files, including photos and files of drawings or "clip art").
- Presentation software (to prepare materials as computer presentations, transparencies, or handouts).
- Web site publishing software (for managing the content of your Web site in-house).
- Financial management (to manage invoices, bill dues, and produce basic accounting reports for the board).

Every association should invest in functional association management software (AMS), which typically can handle membership management, dues billing, meetings management, and order processing. Usually based on a client server, AMS applications allow sharing tens or hundreds of thousands of data records and allow many people to use the system simultaneously.

Prices for AMS packages range from a few hundred dollars for a basic program that works on one workstation to tens of thousands of dollars for networked systems with expanded functions. The cost of network AMS systems can easily reach $30,000 to $40,000 or more for software and services.

A small association that lacks funds for expensive AMS programs can build its own database and customize a generic contact management system. Another alternative is to purchase an off-the-shelf AMS solution (for under $1,000) that has all the functionality required in a small office environment. Typically, some data conversion is required, and you should budget for some user training and system configuration or customization.

Remember that a partially automated system is better than a completely manual system. Building it yourself or customizing an off-the-shelf system will still provide some automation at a lower price.

If you plan to produce some of your own publications or manage graphics and photos for your Web site in-house, you'll need to invest in a quality graphics application. You'll also want a solid Web design tool to make your organization look as good online as it does in print. Adobe Photoshop is the gold standard for image editing, and there are several good choices from the likes of Adobe, Corel, Macromedia, and Quark.

If you're managing the content of your Web site, you'll need software to get your text and graphics onto the Web. Look for a basic Web design and publishing tool, and make sure the software you choose is supported by your Web host. Microsoft FrontPage and Macromedia Dreamweaver are arguably the two leading programs for this purpose; both are simple to use.

Finally, your small association must have software to manage its finances. Understand the difference between an accounting package and checkbook software. Your software should be able to create accounting reports, manage payroll taxes, manage invoices, bill dues and, ideally, integrate with your AMS software. The market leaders for this type of software are Intuit QuickBooks, PeachTree, and Microsoft Money.

Go Mobile

You may spend a considerable amount of time out of the office meeting members and attending meetings. To have access to your office while on the road, consider these mobile technology enhancements:

Notebook Computer. Consider a lightweight, portable model that enables you to connect to your office network. The smallest notebooks, known as ultraportables, generally weigh four pounds or less and tend to be less than one inch thick. Thin-and-lights, despite the name, are slightly thicker and heavier; they generally weigh between four and six pounds. Still, they are travel friendly and offer the performance and features of much larger notebooks.

In fact, many of the new notebook computers can be brought into the office and plugged into a docking station, to replace a desktop computer. You can find thin-and-lights with memory measured in gigabytes, huge hard drives, cutting-edge graphics, and combination CD/DVD burners that all but eliminate the need for the second optical drive found in larger mainstream and desktop-replacement systems.

The most significant development in notebook computers was the arrival of Intel's Centrino technology. If you are buying an ultraportable or thin-and-light notebook, start with a Pentium M processor.

Handheld Computer (PDA). More than just electronic organizers, today's handhelds enable you to connect to the Web, check your e-mail, work on office files and, in the case of smart phones, double as your cell phone. In fact, a well-equipped PDA can stand in for a laptop when you're in a pinch.

All handhelds also have an address book, an appointment calendar, a task list, and notes, which you can synchronize with Microsoft Outlook or other popular personal information managers.

The most recent advances in handhelds have been in the area of wireless communications. Bluetooth lets you synchronize wirelessly, exchange files, or connect to other Bluetooth-enabled devices such as cell phones. Wi-Fi lets you access public hot spots or LANs (local area networks) at home or at the office to check e-mail and browse the Web. Finally, wide-area networking uses cellular networks such as GSM/GPRS or CDMA to stay connected over broader areas, albeit at much slower speeds. The latter, also known as smart phones, support voice communications and serve as both PDA and cell phone.

Cellular Telephone. Long battery life is essential. Look for cell phones that use a lithium-ion (Li-ion) battery rather than a nickel-metal-hydride (NiMH). Li-ion batteries weigh less and provide 10 to 20 percent better performance than their NiMH counterparts. You'll want a phone with a rated talk time of at least three and a half hours, preferably closer to five hours. If your mobile comes with a desktop charger, splurge for the travel charger, too; it's significantly smaller and easier to pack for business trips.

If your travels often take you well beyond your home calling area, make sure your cell phone supports analog roaming. Although analog calls are expensive, you'll be guaranteed coverage even in remote rural areas. If you travel overseas, you'll want a GSM (Global System for Mobile communications) phone, which operates on networks (GSM 800/1800/1900) in Europe, Asia, and the United States.

You'll also want a handset that features a hefty address book—at least 300 names with support for multiple entries per contact. Some phones allow you to include information such as e-mail, Web, and street addresses with your contacts. Make sure the phone supports conference calling, just in case you have to conduct an emergency meeting while you're on the road. You may also be interested in two-way, walkie-talkie-style communication.

As your communication needs become more sophisticated, consider investing in the more expensive smart phone technology that combines the functionality of a PDA and cellular phone in one device.

Association success doesn't depend upon a shiny new computer sitting on every desk or the most expensive association management software suite. However, associations should regularly assess what technology is available (within their budgets) to help them meet their technology needs and further the organizational mission, goals, and strategies. Sound management always starts with planning, and your association should regularly assess its technology plan to make sure it is current and reflects your overall business plan.

Association Logos

By Robert E. McLean, CAE

HAVE YOU EVER NOTICED that some associations seem to have a different logo printed on every brochure, manual, or business card, because the colors always seem a shade lighter or darker? While this inconsistency might be traced to a less than professional printing company, it often results from the association failing to develop and use appropriate graphic files or stipulate specific colors.

You can avoid this problem by ensuring that an inventory of essential documents—such as the original incorporation documents, IRS letter of determination, and certificate of authority—include the association's original logo art files.

When developing and using logos in printed materials, on the Web, and in computer-generated programs, such as presentation software, focus on these three issues.

Colors

The simplest explanation for logo variations in printed materials and on Web sites is that the association fails to establish graphic standards for use by in-house or contract artists, designers, and printers. The graphic standards for your association's logo should include a list of the exact colors it includes.

A color logo is often a combination of two, three, or four colors. (Remember that, when working with printing companies, black is counted as a color.) To ensure color consistency you must know the number assigned to the shade of, say, blue or green in your logo.

Printing companies follow the Pantone Matching System (PMS) for ensuring correct, consistent colors in their work. Under this system, hundreds of shades of every color (including black) are each assigned a PMS number. Using PMS colors ensures that the same color appears in a logo on every project, even if many different printing companies are involved.

On the Web, the number of available colors is limited to 216 shades. That's why it's essential when a graphic designer develops or recreates a logo that the association obtains that design in several file types, each designed to work best in a particular medium.

At times, of course, your association's logo will appear in black and white. Therefore, be sure the designer includes a simplified version of the association's logo for such situations.

Graphic File Types

To ensure quality and consistency in the reproduction of your logo, use the right file for each project—and obtain the original graphic software files the artist used to create them (most often a program such as Photoshop).

Here are some of the more popular graphics files and their typical uses:

Tagged Image File Format (.tiff or .tif) files are large and versatile, offering high quality resolution in documents produced with word processing and desktop publishing programs. It is impossible to compress them into small files using software such as WinZip.

Graphics Interchange Format (.gif) and *Joint Photographic Experts Group* (.jpg) files are low-resolution files often used on Web sites. They are easily compressed into small files using software such as WinZip.

Bitmap (.bmp, .rle, .dib) files are small and created only by Microsoft programs such as Word, PowerPoint, and Publisher.

Encapsulated PostScript (.eps) files are large, complex files preferred by graphic designers who want to ensure high-quality reproduction, such as when sending materials to a printing company. Word processing and desktop publishing documents with PostScript images may require special printers that can handle the PostScript programming language.

Legal Protection

Your association's logo is an important piece of intellectual property that must be protected to ensure that no other association or company uses it or creates a design that is nearly identical. That process begins by signing a contract with the graphic designer who develops the logo, making it clear that your association owns the final product.

Once your designer produces the finished art, consider further legal protection for your logo by applying for a trademark. The United States Patent and Trademark Office (USPTO) defines a trademark as a word, name, symbol, or device used in trade with goods to indicate the source of the goods and to distinguish them from the goods of others. Trademarks can be renewed forever as long as they are being used in commerce.

You can obtain information on the registration procedure for trademarks and use the Trademark Electronic Application System (TEAS) available online at www.uspto.gov/teas/index.html. (If you prefer to submit a paper application to the USPTO, call 800-786-9199 to obtain a printed form; mail it to the Commissioner for Trademarks, 2900 Crystal Dr., Arlington, VA 22202-3514.)

It's All a Matter of Record

By Shirley L. Nimsky

E VEN FOR THE SMALL association, record keeping and filing can be arduous and challenging without an overall plan for handling the paperwork. The plan need not be complex; however, it should be consistent and logical so that the various records and files can be easily found for presentation, duplication, and auditing.

Good records management provides for

- Faster retrieval of information for the staff who work with records.
- Control of the life cycle of records.
- Compliance with administrative legal and fiscal requirements.
- Fewer lost or misplaced records.
- Protection for the association's vital and historical records.
- Easier decision making regarding potential expenditures and space planning for physical and electronic document storage.

The types of records in an association office could possibly be divided into (but not limited to) the following categories, depending on the organizational and staff needs.

Administration

Board/Committees
- Rosters
- Minutes of boards, committees, and general assemblies with members; records of all actions approved by members

- Resolutions adopted by board of directors relating to characteristics, qualifications, rights limitations, and obligations of members or any class of category of members
- Correspondence to members

Bylaws, Rules, and Regulations

Member Records

- Application form
- Acceptance/welcome correspondence
- Important membership information such as ID, passwords, rules, requirements
- Correspondence directly related to member or member records, organizational participation, and volunteering

Salary Administration

- Payroll processing information
- W-2
- W-4
- Payroll history
- Payroll checks
- Personnel action forms
- Time sheets
- Workers compensation
- Federal, state, and local tax records and reports

Accounts Payable

- Vouchers with documentation for:
  - Bills
  - Credit card statements
  - Credit card charge slips
  - Invoices
  - Expense reports
  - Travel expense reports
- 1099s

Audit Reports

- Financial reports from auditor
- Trial balance
- Income statements

- Balance sheet
- Consolidated financial statements

General Accounting

- Accounting procedures
- Charts of accounts
- Batch documentation
- Daily revenue reconciliation

Banking

- Bank deposits
- Monthly statements with reconciliations
- Check registers
- Cancelled checks
- Deposits slips
- Wire transfers

Budget

- Budget documents
- Documentation of review

Capital Property

- Capital assets records
- Equipment leases
- Software licenses
- Depreciation schedules

Insurance Management

- Organizational policies
- Injury/accident reports
- Liability insurance policies

Human Resources Records

These should be handled and filed separately as suggested below. Be sure to check local, state, and federal guidelines for handling employment documentation and records.

- Employment information.

* Applications and resumes (typically kept for one year then destroyed).
* Performance reviews
* Disciplinary actions and training records
* Position descriptions
* Separation forms
* Offer letters
* Employment contracts

- I-9 Forms. Although not required to be kept separate, it may be convenient if requested by the Department of Labor inspectors. If your association is responsible for its own payroll, keep these documents with tax withholding records.
- Equal Employment Opportunity (EEO) records. By law, these documents may not be used for employment status issues; keep them separate from the employee's record.
- Medical information, such as employment health exams and workers' compensation medical evaluations.

The length of time you need to keep personnel records varies by state law. Here are recommended minimum lengths:

- Basic employee information (including I-9): Four years from termination.
- Payroll and benefits information: five years.
- Employment actions (firing, demotions, promotions): four years.
- Job-related illnesses and injuries: five years.
- Medical exams: 30 years.
- Toxic substance and blood-borne pathogen exposure records: 30 years.

Policy and Procedure Documents
- Policy manuals
- Procedure manuals and guidelines

Correspondence
- Letters
- E-mail
- Newsletters

Legal

- Licenses
- Contracts
- Articles and restated articles of incorporation
- List of names and address of current directors and officers
- Annual reports delivered to Secretary of State, Corporation Commission, or applicable jurisdiction
- Other corporate legal documents
- Proxies
- Disciplinary hearing committee files
- State tax-exempt records
- State registrations of corporate name
- Federal exemption records
- Copyright and intellectual property

Technology has made it possible for associations to cut down on the amount of paperwork retained physically in the office through the use of digital scanning and storage. Using this method of storing documents and files may depend upon local, state, and federal statutory regulations; the availability and cost of storage space; retrieval needs; and personnel resources.

Selecting a Contract Lobbyist

By Diana Ewert, CAE

MICRO-STAFF ORGANIZATIONS WITH EXECUTIVES and staff already wearing many hats may opt to augment their legislative services with a contract lobbyist. This person can provide myriad services, such as direct lobbying of a specific issue; crafting legislation to better the profession; developing policy statements; providing testimony; or even serving as an auditor to keep the organization informed of pending legislation, hearings, or committee meetings.

You've probably heard a horror story or two about lobbyists who damage the organization's reputation through misinformation, miscommunication, or just not doing the job. So how do you find the right lobbyist for your association? Here are some tips:

- If you are looking for a lobbyist to fill a need from a state perspective, start with the state's ethics Web page. Most states have a Web-based program where you can look up lobbyists by name or by client. See who is providing services to organizations similar to your own. If you will be advocating in front of specific committees that handle your issues, find out which legislators serve on these committees. You can then have your member constituents talk to the legislators and find out which lobbyists are effective and have good reputations.

- Start building a list of individuals or firms that will receive your request for proposal (RFP) for legislative services. Send the RFP to all those you believe can provide the service, and don't be surprised to receive calls requesting an RFP once the word is out that you are looking (the contract lobby community is very tight knit). The RFP will contain a list of services to be performed and may contain the amount you anticipate spending for those services. Include any meetings you may wish the lobbyist to attend to give briefings to members, as well as the reporting relationship. Be sure that all parties understand the lobbyist will report to the executive rather than a volunteer leader. (See Appendix A for a sample RFP.)

• Look for a lobbyist *before* the legislative session begins. Don't wait until you have a hot issue in the middle of the session—when responses to your RFP may be lower and prices for the services may be substantially higher.

• Once you have received responses to the RFP, start checking references. Don't hesitate to call clients and discuss the lobbyist's performance. Be sure to look at the client list to identify potential conflicts of interest. If some exist, make sure you understand how the individual or firm will handle them.

• Develop a list of the top three to five candidates, and invite them to make a presentation to the selection committee or the board of directors. The purpose of the presentation is to see how the individuals relate to the volunteer leaders, the executive, and the staff. Weigh the responses of the executive and staff carefully: These are the two groups that will be involved when an issue requires an immediate response.

• Once you have selected a lobbyist and signed the contract, have the lobbyist spend some time at the office getting acquainted with staff and getting educated about the organization. Prioritize the issues of the coming session, and provide background information such as reports, white papers, and other data that will enable the contractor to do the best job. This is an opportune time to begin building a relationship among the executive, staff, and lobbyist.

• Delineate the appropriate lines of communication when "hot issues" arise during the session. For example, what happens if the executive is out of reach and testimony needs to be provided the following day on an issue that the organization supports or opposes? Anticipate the unexpected as much as possible.

• Build in an evaluation of the work being performed. Evaluation is essential to the ongoing relationship you are building. It can take two or three sessions before a contract lobbyist fully understands your issues and can effectively communicate your viewpoint to legislators.

Taking Stock

By Jimelle F. Rumberg, CAE

BORING AS IT MAY seem, inventory is a necessity—especially for small staff associations that can't afford to overspend on needless supplies. Storage space is always at a premium for associations, no matter what their size, so organize to economize. Whether you perform inventory at the end of your fiscal year, calendar year, or a rolling-six month period, periodically purge your files of unnecessary paper, shred, and recycle to conserve space.

When cataloging your publications, consider saving five copies of each issue and disposing of any extras after one year. Label and file audiotapes, videotapes, floppies, and CDs; list them, as well as books, in a database for tracking purposes. December is usually a good time to update the database with tapes and books purchased throughout the year. Also perform year-end back-ups of data.

If your association prints membership certificates, continuing education (CE) certificates, and award certificates using specialty papers, do an annual inventory to assess paper needs for future projects. When paper becomes old, it absorbs moisture and misfeeds in the copier so, if you order an extra case or two of paper because it's on sale, make sure to store it off the floor, on a pallet or shelf, and close to a dehumidifier to stay "fresh."

Count on-hand stock of membership pins and name badge holders so you don't run low before conventions. If you have two main events per year, inventory name badges and ribbons twice yearly. Also consider recycling the name badge holders by placing a "We recycle" sign and collection box at the registration table. Members will appreciate your thriftiness and, with a fresh insert, most of the badges can be used again.

Speaking of conventions, don't forget to inventory left-over gift items every year. When filled with candy, pens, or other goodies, coffee mugs and desk boxes carrying the association's logo make great gifts for new student members, speakers, or volunteers. Re-order during price-deals or overstock specials—but remember that shipping and logo imprinting add dramatically to the per-piece cost.

It's good office practice to know what's on your shelves. So get in the habit of scheduling a casual day once a year to take stock of what you have. Here's a basic list of what to inventory:

Basic Supplies
- Letterhead
- Second page letterhead or plain paper
- #10 envelopes
- Large (shipping) envelopes
- Shipping labels
- Business cards (for staff and officers)
- Copy paper
- Officer or member pins
- PAC supporter pins
- Membership certificates
- Emblem items (mugs, t-shirts, jackets)
- Backup media (disks or tapes)
- Emergency preparedness and first-aid materials
- File folders and hanging folders
- Name badges
- Name badge holders
- Writing pens and pencils
- Membership brochures, recruitment materials

Meeting Planner Essentials
- Antiseptic wipes
- First aid kit with bandages
- Bottle of water
- Breakfast or energy bars
- Cash for tipping
- Cell phone and charger
- Dental floss (unbreakable thread for buttons or use as twine)

- Duct, clear, and masking tape
- Extra name badges
- Hand wipes
- Important phone numbers
- Jacket or sweater
- Box cutter/utility knife
- Markers (black, colors)
- Mints or gum
- Notepad/sticky notes
- Index cards
- Laser pointer
- Rubber bands
- Scissors
- Small tool kit with screwdrivers (flat head and Phillips)
- Extra file folders
- Staple remover, stapler, and staples
- Tissues
- Plastic storage bags
- 3-hole punch
- Extension cord
- Collapsible dolly
- CD-Rs, floppy disks
- Extra batteries (AA and AAA)
- Extra tough trash bags
- Retractable measuring tape
- Telephone cord
- Umbrella
- Spare USB cord
- Antacid tablets
- Aspirin/ibuprofen
- Binder clips
- Ruler
- Sharpie pens
- Hand lotion
- Velcro
- Correction fluid
- Power strip
- Flashlight

- Mending kit
- Safety pins
- Receipt book
- Pens/pencils/pencil sharpener
- Highlighters
- Calculator
- #10 Envelopes
- Packing and shipping materials
- Local telephone book
- Chalk and eraser/dry markers
- Disposable camera
- Canvas gardening gloves (for unloading boxes)
- Spray adhesive/rubber cement
- Other

Checklist for Printing Promotional Pieces

By Jimelle F. Rumberg, CAE

IMAGINE LEAVING OUT AN important piece of information—such as the meeting site's name—when printing a large run of promotional materials for an educational event, party, meeting, or conference. Not only is the error embarrassing but you'll also have to field all the calls from members who need the information.

To avoid such a mistake, here is a comprehensive list of the details you should include in your association's promotional pieces:

- Course title
- Benefit statement
- Course objectives and descriptions
- Faculty and biographical information
- Date, time, and location
- Registrations fees (including deadline for discount, if applicable)
- Credits available to attendees
- Course schedule
- Teaching methods (lecture, panel, etc.)
- Intended audience level of instruction for attendees (beginner, intermediate, advanced)
- Registration forms
- Enrollment limit
- ADA disclaimer
- Policy on course cancellation
- Hotel information, room blocks, special rates for meeting
- Any special feature (across from shopping mall, parks, theaters, etc.)
- A well-balanced and appealing design

- The association's logo (identifiable and prominent)
- An attention-getting graphic or symbol
- Convincing language; proper grammar
- Appropriate emotional appeal
- An opportunity to see immediate application for program content
- Information sufficient for a decision to register *now*
- A request for action
- An inducement to act (early-bird registration or discounts)
- An opportunity to act (register online; by fax; by phone)

Looking Out for Your Successor

By Tom Holt, CAE

O NE OF THE NICEST things that my predecessor did for me was to leave in his desk a sealed envelope containing two memos, which included information ranging from the vital to the helpful. Those two memos were of enormous help to me as I took the helm of an organization about which I knew little. I referred to them often during the first few months, and again when I prepared the next year's budget to get a feel for what had changed.

Planning for the Worst

I recalled those valuable memos after the events of September 11, 2001, when disaster planning suddenly became everyone's priority. Using my predecessor's memos as a reference, I prepared a *disaster file* to keep in my desk.

The memos that I prepared are in a sealed envelope addressed "To the Next Executive Director." The file contains essential information that other executives may want to consider recording:

- Passwords for computers and any other equipment.
- Names of people to notify in the event of incapacity or death.
- Lists of bank accounts and credit cards.
- Key members and industry partners who could be counted on for sound advice and assistance.

I update the memos about once a year, an exercise that helps me to evaluate our progress on organizational goals. That's already a part of our annual planning meeting, of course, but updating the disaster file provides a different perspective. It forces me to ask, "What are the really top priorities?"

Departing on Schedule

For a planned transition, you can be even more detailed. The two memos that my predecessor left me included a great deal of invaluable information, both concrete and analytical. They included:

Key budget numbers—One memo was a detailed annotation of the budget. It also outlined a bit of financial history and highlighted areas subject to significant change due to industry trends or external forces. That memo helped me quickly gain an understanding of both potential financial land mines and opportunities.

General organizational brief—The second memo was a candid organizational brief. It included

- Tips about the incumbent staff's strengths and weaknesses (something that ideally should be in written evaluations).
- Key volunteer and associate member contacts.
- A summary of important organizational issues.

Also create a list of your unwritten, yet vital, policies and procedures and put them in writing. Such random policies will vary from organization to organization, so it's important to brainstorm. For instance, if you operate a political action committee, create a list of state compliance tips (for example, it is imperative that, in Oregon, the state be notified when a new treasurer is appointed).

Whether your departure is planned or unplanned, preparing for your successor will allow him or her to immediately focus on moving the organization forward instead of fretting about back-office details. You may even find that the process of planning for tomorrow will serve your organization today.

This article originally appeared in the July 2004 issue of Association Management, *published by the American Society of Association Executives, Washington, D.C., and is reprinted with permission.*

Request for Legislative Services

Provided by the Missouri Academy of Family Physicians, Kansas City. Reprinted with permission.

MISSOURI ACADEMY OF FAMILY PHYSICIANS

Background

The Missouri Academy of Family Physicians is a 501(c)(6) individual membership organization founded in 1947 with approximately 1,750 members across the state. The membership base is comprised of family practice physicians—those actively practicing medicine—residents, students, and academicians. The goal of the Academy in its involvement with the state legislative process is one of "patient advocacy." The Academy reviews legislation in the context of the impact to the delivery of quality healthcare for all of Missouri's citizens. This legislation includes issues dealing with scope of practice, Medicaid, formulary, access to care and coverage of care to name a few. The long term goal of the Academy is to achieve quality health care for all. In seeking this goal, the Academy has a well respected reputation of placing patient interests ahead of all else.

As an affiliated chapter of the American Academy of Family Physicians, the Missouri Academy refers to the policy statements of AAFP first for general direction. The American Academy of Family Physicians Government Affairs Commission then reviews the issue as interpreted in the state and further refines the policy specific to Missouri.

The Academy staff is 3.5 FTE including an executive director, director of finance and operations, membership coordinator and foundation coordinator. The office is housed in Kansas City with the executive director actively engaged in legislative and regulatory outreach efforts in Jefferson City and around the state. The Academy has contracted with a lobbyist for services for the last six years. With the executive director now a registered lobbyist in Missouri, the Academy seeks an even more active legislative voice in Jefferson City utilizing the executive director in collaboration with a contract lobbyist. The Academy will open a satellite office in Jefferson City to facilitate and coordinate its advocacy efforts.

Scope of Services

Prior to the start of the General Assembly session, the firm or individual will work with the Missouri Academy officers, Government Affairs Commission, and executive director to develop a legislative agenda. Services provided may include but are not limited to:

1. Monitoring of proposed legislation, rules, regulations, policies and procedures which may have an impact on patient care in Missouri.

2. Identification of stakeholders and their positions; history on proposed legislation, if any; legislators who support/oppose; and notification of hearings.

3. Provide an introduction and/or arrange for meetings with key legislators, appointed officials, employees, departments, division, agencies or boards or commissions of the executive branch of the government concerning legislation which may have an impact on patient care in Missouri.

4. Provide a weekly written report to the Executive Director, Board of Directors and Commission on Government Affairs regarding legislative developments and activities.

5. Advise Missouri Academy of legislative hearings and meetings where Missouri Academy input is needed.

6. Attend Academy board and commission meetings as requested (up to four each year).

7. Participate in conference calls as requested (up to 12 per legislative session).

8. Be reasonably available for advice and opinion.

This contract position will report to the Academy's executive director who, in turn, reports to the Academy Board of Directors and is staff liaison for the Government Affairs Commission.

Length of Contract

The contract will be for a 12-month period beginning _____.
Either side may agree to terminate the contract with thirty (30) days advance notice at any time without any further payments required.

Budget

While the Academy has a preliminary budget of $_____ for this legislative activity, we ask that the proposal include a fee schedule, both hourly and lump sum, for each of the items listed under the Scope of Services.

The final budget and activities will be determined by the Academy's Executive Commission and voted on by the Academy's Board of Directors.

Proposal

In order for the Missouri Academy to make a qualified selection, the individual or firm must submit:

1. A cover letter expressing interest in this matter, including an understanding of the engagement and, if a firm, the responsible firm members.

2. A fee schedule (both hourly and lump sum) for each of the items listed under Scope of Services.

3. A curriculum vitae or other resume of experience and expertise.

4. A list of clients including disclosure of potential conflicts of interest and how such conflicts will be resolved.

5. A description of previous experience with the Governor's office, Office of Administration, Department of Health and Senior Services and other health care executive and regulatory offices/departments.

The proposal should be submitted to the Missouri Academy of Family Physicians by mail, fax or e-mail (with a hard copy to follow) to _____.

The Executive Commission will review the submissions and invite the selected finalists to present a proposal at the Missouri Academy Executive Commission meeting on _____.

CD-ROM Contents

Articles
- "Checklist for Printing Promotional Pieces" by Jimelle F. Rumberg, CAE
- "Taking Stock" inventory lists by Jimelle F. Rumberg, CAE

Forms
- Executive Director Evaluation Form
- Leadership Contract
- Multiple Monthly Duties Calendar
- Sample Administrative Calendar

Meeting Planning Forms
- Annual Convention Budget Worksheet
- Annual Convention Event History Form
- Annual Convention Sample RFP
- Banquet Event Order
- Conference Evaluation Form
- Conference Speaker Information Confirmation
- Convention Monitor Training Handout
- Event Function Sheet
- Sample Hotel Rooming List
- Session Monitor's Checklist
- Speaker Agreement Form
- Speaker Guidelines
- Speaker Biographical and Seminar Information
- Speaker Meeting Room Requirements
- Speaker Housing and Travel Arrangements
- Speaker Reimbursement Policies
- Speaker Request Form
- Statement for Professional Services

ASAE & The Center for Association Leadership

ASAE & The Center for Association Leadership are two organizations working together to create the most comprehensive collection of resources, educational opportunities and advocacy for association professionals. ASAE contributes significant association management knowledge and resources while the Center for Association Leadership supplies unmatched learning, future-focused research and knowledge resources to create an organization that offers association professionals an impressive array of essential services and resources for today and tomorrow. The organizations are dedicated to providing association professionals with the essential resources they need for professional success.

ASAE & The Center for Association Leadership:
Our Brand Promise

We promise to provide great experiences, a vibrant community, and essential tools that make you and your organization more successful.

Types of Members

There are two types of ASAE members: association executives and business partners. All members join professional-interest sections that relate to their job responsibilities. Sections include:

- Association management company
- Component relations
- Communication
- Executive management
- Finance & business operations
- Government relations
- International
- Legal
- Marketing
- Meetings and expositions
- Membership
- Professional development
- Technology

For more information

Contact ASAE & The Center for Association Leadership by phone at 202-626-2723; by fax at 202-371-8315; by e-mail at **service@asaenet.org**, or visit **www.asaenet.org** for more information on programs and services available from ASAE.